Janet Vogelsang, MSW, BCD

The Witness Stand
A Guide for Clinical Social Workers in the Courtroom

Pre-publication
REVIEWS,
COMMENTARIES,
EVALUATIONS . . .

"*The Witness Stand* is a gem of useful information for the expert in the courtroom. I wish I had earlier access to the commonsense information Janet Vogelsang presents. I would have been much better prepared for my initial courtroom experiences. I am sure my preparation and testimony in court would have gone much smoother. Preparing for court and testimony can be a daunting task at times. This book helps one develop an organized approach in courtroom preparation. These useful ideas will help remind every expert witness about crucial points before testimony. Vogelsang's book helps put the legal process in perspective and I find her approach very reassuring. She reveals her own anxieties and fears about the courtroom and how she has handled them.

The book is arranged in pertinent sections with useful summaries at the end of each chapter. Vogelsang expresses herself clearly with a light sense of humor. Her emphasis on proper preparation is essential and the discussion of courtroom dynamics is quite enlightening."

W. Alexander Morton, PharmD, BCPP
Professor of Pharmacy Practice,
Associate Professor of Psychiatry
and Behavioral Sciences,
Medical University of South Carolina,
Charleston

"*The Witness Stand* is such a helpful guide to any professional who is involved in the legal and courtroom process. Janet Vogelsang's depth of experience and writing style make for a very readable and essential source for clinicians at any level of practice."

Elaine Smith, MSW
Clinical Social Worker,
Private Practice,
Greenville, South Carolina

More pre-publication
REVIEWS, COMMENTARIES, EVALUATIONS . . .

"*The Witness Stand* is a rich compendium of insights and information for the practicing clinical social worker. Often we, as a profession, feel intimidated by the court experience, but the author helps to allay anxiety by stating that 'we are simply there to report what we have learned.'

The importance of being thorough and thoughtful in our assessment using psychosocial methods is reinforced throughout the book, with multiple resources offered to aid in structuring our evaluation of the client. The Checklist for Investigations, one of many useful forms included in the book, is a primer of the issues and ethics surrounding discovery."

Gail Nagel, MS, BCD
President,
American Board of Examiners
in Clinical Social Work Inc.

"*The Witness Stand*, by Janet Vogelsang, furnishes an invaluable beacon for social workers whose professional efforts lead to testimony, often in criminal cases. Vogelsang is experienced and articulate, a good guide for the social worker who is uncertain and possibly intimidated in dealings with lawyers in and outside of the courtroom. From my perspective as a neurologist, this book is most helpful in spelling out what a social worker must do to provide a comprehensive assessment of the psychosocial background of the subject. It identifies what I must know about the social matrix from which the criminal springs."

Jonathan H. Pincus, MD
Professor of Neurology,
Chairman Emeritus of Neurology,
Georgetown University
School of Medicine,
Washington, DC

"One feature that makes this book so useful is that it was written by a social worker for social workers. It is evident that the author speaks from vast personal experience in writing this guide for clinical social workers in the courtroom. The book reflects Vogelsang's strong educational background, her understanding of social work theory, her years of professional practice, and her belief in and commitment to the field of social work. These qualities have enabled her to produce a book that is well written, highly informative, and interesting to read.

Ms. Vogelsang provides numerous helpful hints throughout the book. For example, she describes how to deal with the anxiety of testifying, how to respond to cross-examination, and how to qualify as an expert witness without becoming defensive. She also discusses appropriate courtroom demeanor, the use of visual aids, and tips for testifying in court. The summary lists at the end of each chapter are especially helpful.

This book will be extremely useful to all social workers who will be called upon to testify in court. It will also be helpful to agency directors and supervisors, social work educators, and social work students. It addresses an important area that has received scant attention in social work literature, and does so in a manner that is educational and, at the same time, entertaining."

Dr. Frank B. Raymond III, PhD
Professor/Dean,
College of Social Work,
University of South Carolina

The Witness Stand
A Guide for Clinical Social Workers in the Courtroom

The Witness Stand
A Guide for Clinical Social Workers in the Courtroom

Janet Vogelsang, MSW, BCD

The Haworth Social Work Practice Press
An Imprint of The Haworth Press, Inc.
New York • London • Oxford

Published by

The Haworth Social Work Practice Press, an imprint of The Haworth Press, Inc., 10 Alice Street, Binghamton, NY 13904-1580

Cover design by Jennifer M. Gaska.

Library of Congress Cataloging-in-Publication Data

Vogelsang, Janet.
    The witness stand : a guide for clinical social workers in the courtroom / Janet Vogelsang.
       p. cm.
    Includes bibliographical references and index.
    ISBN 0-7890-1144-1 (hard : alk. paper)—ISBN 0-7890-1145-X (soft : alk. paper)
    1. Evidence, Expert—United States. 2. Psychology, Forensic—United States. 3. Psychiatric social work—United States. 4. Social workers—United States. I. Title.

KF8965 .V64 2001
347.73′67—dc21
                                                                         00-050549

CONTENTS

ABOUT THE AUTHOR

Janet Vogelsang, MSW, BCD, is in private practice in Greenville, South Carolina, where she conducts biopsychosocial assessments and testifies in various kinds of court cases such as child custody, termination of parental rights, child abuse, and family violence. She was an advisor on the *Crime Victim's Handbook,* produced by the Office of Victim Assistance, Thirteenth Judicial Circuit in Greenville. She has received official recognition for her outstanding service from the Office of the Thirteenth Circuit Solicitor. She is currently President of the National Association of Social Workers–South Carolina Chapter.

Foreword

Clinical social workers are often profoundly disturbed and indignant about being subpoenaed, as are other professionals. For that reason this book, *The Witness Stand* by Jan Vogelsang, is welcomed and needed. Her fearful fantasy of the judge yelling at her, "Lady, that is the stupidest thing I ever heard in my whole life. Baliff, take her away!" is similar to the fears of many social workers.

This book is the first resource I know of that has been written just for the clinical social worker. In the book, Vogelsang starts where many authors do, with advice on handling specific direct and cross-examination questions. However, she goes well beyond that obvious issue.

Anxiety, angry resentment, and detachment are the three most common emotional states described by expert witnesses who are called to the witness stand. Anxiety clearly predominates in the courtroom. Experts are often apprehensive about being unprepared, and they are jagged-edge anxious that opposing counsels will make fools of them. These anxieties are sometimes obvious: voices quaver, hands shake, and listening skills deteriorate. Narrative answers are interspersed with disfluencies such as "um" and "ah." Topics change in midsentence. Persons with organized and lucid explanations of their findings in congenial settings sound confused and inconsistent.

Angry resentment is most frequently seen in witnesses who are involuntary participants in the legal process, and in witnesses who feel that the adversarial process has demeaned them professionally and distorted their findings and conclusions. Anger and resentment appear often in treating experts. That is, persons who have been offering mental health services to an adult or child may be called as witnesses in child custody hearings, personal injury litigation, and presentence hearings.

The anger and resentment occurs because of conflicting roles. On the one hand, these treating experts have compelling responsibilities to help their clients. On the other hand, they are asked to offer truthful reports in court that may harm the well-being of these same clients. Therapists resent being in that position, and are angry that they have been subpoenaed and required to compromise what they see as a core professional commitment. I do not agree that the responsibility for helping the client is necessarily the first and core priority; the demands of social justice come first. But I absolutely understand the ferocity of the anger that accompanies what seems to be this forced betrayal of the therapeutic alliance.

The third common emotional state for testifying experts is cool detachment. Emotions are subdued most often among mental health experts who are in court regularly for routine, minimally contested legal issues, such as involuntary commitment. These experts are matter of fact, and the proceedings are predictable and repetitive.

All three categories of emotional reactions seem to be increasing because of an ongoing social process in which mental health professionals are brought into many forms of litigation. At one time, social workers, psychologists, and psychiatrists could expect that they could go through their careers with few or no demands to testify. That has changed. Even graduate students and professionals who avoid courses and placements involving the law find that there is no quiet refuge from the insistent demands of the courts. Because mental health professions are widely involved in many areas of family and personal functioning, the law calls on them. Furthermore, the reach of litigation often extends to the results of ordinary diagnostic and treatment activities. "Be prepared" is more than just the Boy Scouts' motto.

No data exist to indicate what professions are most affected. However, my expert witness workshops always have a large number of clinical social workers who fall into the angry resentment category. Anxiety cuts across professional fields, as does detachment.

Vogelsang provides three strategies in this book for testifying social workers that are available in no other source. First, she develops the presentation of the results of biopsychosocial assessments in expert testimony. The book speaks to the essential issues to be addressed and the ways in which to discuss them.

Second, Vogelsang offers a discussion of how to work with investigators and use their information in court testimony. Investigators are present and important in the planning and case development of many attorneys. Most of us who testify value what investigators do, but testify only to our findings. Vogelsang takes investigators' knowledge to the next step, drawing on how to use their talents and results.

Finally, Vogelsang reviews affidavits. No one ever taught me how to prepare an affidavit. Yet, like many other experts, I am frequently asked to submit one. This book helps the expert think about and prepare for this possibility.

Social workers who testify in court need a book that applies to their own work and discipline. Instead, they must read books by psychologists, psychiatrists, and lawyers, and then extrapolate the information to their testimonies. With the publication of this book, clinical social workers now have a professional sourcebook that speaks to their needs regarding preparation for court cases, and how to testify. It is a timely and meaningful contribution.

Stanley L. Brodsky
Department of Psychology
University of Alabama
Tuscaloosa, Alabama
Author of Testifying in Court

Acknowledgments

Appreciation for the thoughtful analysis of the original manuscript goes to Ruth Friedman, Ellen Luepker, Devin Brown, and Stanley Brodsky. Technical assistance provided by John Gilfoil was invaluable.

Gratitude for their unerring support belongs to my family and especially my husband, Grant Hursey.

Introduction

Graduate school taught me that no courses are offered on the role of the clinical social worker in the courtroom, nor do I recall any sort of auxiliary texts having been suggested. Except for one half-day class at the Los Angeles Department of Public Social Services, where I had my first job as a caseworker, no preparation was presented for courtroom testimony. Unquestionably, this is a void that needs to be filled. After fifteen years of conducting biopsychosocial assessments and testifying in court, I have drawn some conclusions about clinical social worker preparation and the witness stand. When preparing testimony for court, I draft my conclusions first. I then go through the volumes of information obtained, and begin the process of testing whether those conclusions are valid. Since this method has always worked well for me, this book starts with conclusions drawn during the course of my witness stand experiences. Humor has been injected throughout, as one of many necessary tools for helping to lower anxiety about testifying in court.

CONCLUSIONS ABOUT THE WITNESS STAND

Most professionals fear the witness stand. Medical doctors claim to hate lawyers, but I suspect that at least part of that dislike is displaced fear the doctors have of the witness stand. Psychologists grin and bear it because their test results are important and they tend to stay focused on the myriad scales, graphs, standard deviations, and such. I envy their ability to be humorous at the right moment during testimony. Clinical social workers march bravely to the stand like martyrs about to be burned at the stake, as they continue their 100-year history of going to court, knowing the witness stand is a tough location.

The courtroom creates anxiety and its accompanying symptoms such as sweaty palms, stomach cramps, flushed skin, racing heart, frozen vocal chords, faintness, shortness of breath, and dry mouth. This of course leads to a sense of being totally out of control and can turn into panic. Some lawyers run to the rest room to throw up during the course of a trial. Others must change shirts, socks, and blouses once or twice a day during legal proceedings. I find this strangely comforting. "Great! It isn't just me. We all feel a little shaky," exclaims the voice inside my head.

The criminal justice system is not an orderly, logical, or seemingly fair system but one that appears chaotic, rushed, and filled with dilemmas. Even the lawyers and judges seem confused at times, which can either lower your anxiety (Whew! They are just as baffled as I am), or increase it (God, help me please! My mind has gone blank and I don't remember a thing. I can't even identify the client!). It takes a few trips to the courtroom to get accustomed to this environment and to prepare well for it.

Then there are those instances when a case is resolved before the trial ever begins (sometimes in the hallway outside the courtroom). First comes a wave of relief as the stress and pressure begin to dissolve, and the adrenaline flow comes to a dizzying stop. Then as you walk to your car, you feel an embarrassing flash of disappointment because you did not get to demonstrate all that hard work!

Clinical social workers are comfortable advocating for clients in war-torn countries, violent neighborhoods, and abusive homes, but mention the witness stand and you get the frozen stare or startled response that indicates the onset of trauma. Fight or flight mode (usually flight) sets in, and you watch as the potential victim edges toward the door. As clinical social workers we go to more places where bullets fly and see more action than many men and women in the armed forces. Studies show that we are at high risk to be harmed while at our work. Yet the courtroom holds many of us at bay even when we want to advocate for our clients.

Know this without one degree of uncertainty: *Clinical social workers belong in a courtroom and the courts need clinical social workers because we have specialized training in conducting biopsychosocial assessments that provide the courts with comprehensive information they are unlikely to hear otherwise.*

Jurors have stated consistently that they understand the clinical social worker better than the doctor, the psychiatrist, the psychologist, the lawyer, the judge and his or her jury instructions, and other professional witnesses. Why? From the time we enter a school of social work, we are taught to be sensitive to culture, language, economic status, disabilities and capabilities, developmental issues, environmental issues, and life experiences. These serve us well as we communicate our ideas in court. We are also trained to take volumes of information from records, interviews, research, and consultations with other experts and to explain how an individual came to his or her current circumstance or behavior. We use this information to form treatment plans, arrange for resources, intervene, and educate. We use visual aids to demonstrate this information in a way that the client or the juror can understand. We adapt our language to increase understanding and we share all of this with other organizations when called upon to do so. One of those organizations is the court, and the court often asks to hear what we learned about the client. If done properly, this biopsychosocial assessment is so comprehensive that it is difficult to imagine how many legal decisions get made without one.

After years of testifying in court, I am never anxiety-free before approaching the witness stand. At a recent training in trauma response, I volunteered to role-play an anxiety-provoking situation so that the trainer could demonstrate the technique she was teaching. Confidently, I told the audience that I would use the hours spent in the courtroom hallway waiting to be called to the stand as my example of anxious behavior. I described some pacing activity, a cycle of going to the water fountain and then the rest room, obsessively going over my testimony in my head, and all the while trying to appear normal to those milling around me in the hallway.

By the time the instructor finished with me, I was laughing hysterically about a fantasy that popped into my head. I realized that I had a fear of being on the witness stand. I envisioned the judge suddenly standing up, pointing his finger at me and screaming, "Lady, that is the stupidest thing I ever heard in my whole life. Bailiff, take her away." Whereupon the bailiff, after my sentencing for the crime of stupidity, handcuffs me and leads me away in shame.

I am happy to report that my anxiety has lessened since volunteering for that exercise, but it will never disappear completely. When experts say that they have no anxiety about testifying, watch as the perspiration soaks into the tops of their shirt collars!

My goal on the witness stand is to tell the truth, to demonstrate what I know, and to be fair in my assessment. I am anxious to avoid bias and to make sure that any reimbursements do not affect my opinions. The judge and jury must be well informed so they can make good decisions, which leave them feeling comfortable that they have done their best even if they disagree with my opinion. I am anxious to represent clinical social workers well and to leave an image of professionalism and thoroughness.

HOW TO USE THIS BOOK

By this time, you have probably noticed that I frequently mention biopsychosocial assessment as a forensic tool. Emphasis on the biopsychosocial assessment will continue throughout the book, and Chapter 2 is devoted to assessment as one of the most valuable assets from social work training.

Each chapter is designed to address a specific issue in preparing for and going to court. The information will be helpful whether you are going to family, criminal, juvenile, or other types of courts. This book does not address only one particular type of legal proceeding in which the clinical social worker might be involved, rather it attempts to give a description of skills that will be needed for all types of cases. For quick reference, a summary with a highlighted list of suggestions is included at the end of each chapter. These suggestions are a brief review of what you need to remember before testifying. This book will fit comfortably into your briefcase, bookbag, or purse and thus be readily available as your court date nears. Reviewing this information lowers my anxiety and reassures me that I am prepared.

Male and female pronouns are switched in the book, not to confuse, but to remind us that the courtroom is occupied by female as well as male lawyers and judges, experts, jurors, law enforcement officers, and others. The term "clinical social worker" rather than forensic social worker or social worker has been chosen for use throughout this book. There are many case managers or caseworkers throughout the United States who are not trained in social work but call themselves social workers. Most of them are dedicated individuals who do a fine job. I use the term clinical to set apart those social workers with bachelor's or master's degrees and/or doctorates in social work. I believe that those kinds of credentials do define a higher level of training and skills, and I would encourage lawyers to investigate those credentials when searching for a social work expert.

This book will also be beneficial to anyone working as a social worker or caseworker who goes to court occasionally or rarely. It contains information helpful to social service directors and supervisors; agency and institution directors and supervisors; professors in colleges of social work interested in preparing their students for the inevitable visit to the witness stand; and private practitioners. Finally, you will see the term "client" used to describe the individual you have been asked to assess for the court or who may have come to you under other circumstances. If you are in private practice, the client may be someone you have been seeing or who has been referred to you, and for whom legal issues have become a part of their case. For example, you may be seeing a rape victim who has decided to prosecute. This individual would be your client, and the state might request your testimony. You may be working in an agency or mental health center and be served a subpoena to testify regarding your client. In some settings, such as mental health centers and psychiatric hospitals, clients are still called patients. In this book, they will be referred to as clients. Often an attorney will have a client that he wants assessed for some legal reason. She will call you and ask for an evaluation or assessment. This individual would be the attorney's client. Keep in mind that the individual being assessed is referred to here as the client whether yours, the lawyer's, or both.

Along with a little humor, this guide also includes some examples of courtroom situations. I hope this defuses some anxiety and provides a bit of debriefing, even if indirectly. One of the things missing from the courtroom experience is that I seldom hear about the outcome of the case. I am not always present to debrief with the client or the attorneys and other experts on the case. It is important to have someone with whom to share the witness stand experience after the fact, and that support is very important for relieving stress and remembering to laugh at some of the absurdities of it all.

I am certain that I have not covered every single aspect of going to court nor is that the intent of this book. When I speak at workshops and seminars, I enjoy the experiences described by others; I encourage you to write or call with questions or experiences that you would like to see included in future articles or books.

Janet Vogelsang
12 East Earle Street
Greenville, South Carolina 29609
(864) 271-1777

Chapter 1

How the Court System Works

Because the subject of how the court system works could be a book all by itself, the information you are most likely to need as a social work expert is included here. However, if you have a question about the laws, statutes, rules, procedures, or types of courts relevant to your case, do not hesitate to call the attorney on your case for answers, or ask if you can come to his office and use his law library. Most attorneys have a library, or you can go to the law library at your local courthouse.

A good paperback law dictionary can be a handy guide to the language you might encounter when preparing for a case. The *Law Dictionary* by Steven Gifis (1991) is a good choice. States can differ and it is important to familiarize yourself with the procedures in your state. If you plan to testify in another state, ask the attorney for assistance in understanding the rules and procedures in that state.

As a word of caution, if you become too sophisticated about the law, you can inadvertently begin using language in your testimony that is best left to the lawyers and the courts (Brodsky, 1991). I have seen expert witnesses admonished for arguing points of law and taking over the job of the attorney. Learn the basics so that you can be clear in terms of what is expected of you in a particular case. Never argue legal points on the stand (Brodsky, 1991).

TYPES OF COURTS AND RULES OF EVIDENCE

There are many different types of courts with rules governing each one in terms of proceedings, evidence, behavior, and testimony. Most social workers are familiar with criminal or family court but can become involved in cases that take them into magistrate's court, equity court, probate court, or others.

There are statutes and rules that govern how the courts proceed in legal matters. If you visit your local courthouse library (highly recommended), you should find books that have the latest rules governing both your state courts and federal courts. For example, when I last visited my local courthouse library, I found the South Carolina Rules of Court—State and Federal (2000).

Under the South Carolina Rules were the following listings:

- SC Rules of Civil Procedure
- SC Rules of Evidence
- SC Rules of Criminal Procedure
- SC Appellate Court Rules
- SC Rules of Family Court
- SC Administrative and Procedural Rules for Magistrate's Court
- SC Rules of Probate Court
- Administration of Circuit Courts, Family Courts, Miscellaneous and Summary Courts, and other divisions such as the Administrative Law Judge Division and Alternative Dispute Resolution

All you need to do is locate this under your state and find the rules that guide the various types of courts in your state. Under the Federal Rules, you will find sections that deal with local civil and criminal rules of the United States District Court for the district of your state.

State cases come under state jurisdiction and are tried by the state. For example, if someone armed himself and robbed a convenience store, the case would be investigated by the local police and the perpetrator would be prosecuted by the state. The case would be referred to as the *State vs. John Doe*. If the same armed robber walked into a bank and stole money, the case would be brought against him by the federal government since crimes committed against banks are federal crimes. The case would be referred to as the *United States vs. John Doe*.

The first case would be governed by State Rules of Evidence and the second by Federal Rules of Evidence. It is important to check the Rules of Evidence for your state since most of your cases will probably be state cases.

Of special interest to the expert witness in a federal case are the articles under the Rules of Evidence, which describe opinions and expert testimony. Also important to the expert witness is the article that guides hearsay testimony. Under the Federal Rules, Rules 702 and 703 describe testimony by experts and bases of opinion testimony by experts. Rule 802 describes hearsay testimony.

In case some of the legal documents you have received for review are confusing to you or if you just want to familiarize yourself with the multitude of legal documents, there is a section in this book containing forms used in various procedures. Among the many examples given, are a Notice of Default Judgment, a Request for Hearing, an Affidavit of Plaintiff, and many others.

TYPES OF WITNESSES

The Rules of Evidence also describe types of witnesses and what they can do. The term "eyewitness" is most often used to define someone who is present at an event and sees or hears what happened firsthand. Eyewitnesses are often called "lay witnesses." Social workers are frequently called upon as lay witnesses especially when they were present to observe personally the events surrounding a case in which they are involved. A lay witness is one who is not testifying as an expert and is not giving an opinion. Lay witness testimony is defined in the Federal Rules of Evidence 701.

Expert witnesses are those who have special knowledge of the subject about the expert is to testify (Gifis, 1991). This is knowledge that would not normally be possessed by the average person. The Federal Rules of Evidence that govern expert witnesses are rules 702, 703, 704, 705, and 706. State rules are often the same or similar but should be checked depending on the case. For example, hearsay rules for experts can differ on the federal level from those on the state level.

AMERICAN JURISPRUDENCE PROOF OF FACTS

Another helpful set of books is available in the courthouse law library. The American Jurisprudence Proof of Facts volumes provide the best examples of good, basic direct examination questions. Different lawyers have written different sections of these books, which address every type of case.

An index is provided for the many volumes of these informative books. The procedure for your case might be:

1. Locate the American Jurisprudence Proof of Facts volumes in the library.
2. Look in the index for the subject of your case, for example, child neglect.
3. Under child neglect you will see some numbers that might read 3POF 2nd, 260, 26-33.
4. Look down the row of volumes until you find 3POF, second series.
5. Look at the top right corner page numbers to find section 260. It will actually read 3-260 to indicate the third volume.
6. In sections 26-33, you will find actual social work testimony in a child neglect case (American Jurisprudence Proof of Facts, 1997).

These sections also give child neglect testimony examples by physicians, teachers, psychologists, and others. Reviewing this not only helps you anticipate the kinds of questions you can expect to be asked, but you can also point out this information to a not-so-aware attorney who is struggling with the appropriate questions in this type of case.

The chapters begin with a description of the fact at issue, related Proof of Facts references, the background information assumed regarding neglected children, judicial standards for intervention, and elements of proof for physical, emotional, and medical neglect. Guides and checklists of facts and circumstances to consider in preparing the case are also available. Included in these volumes are the same kinds of information on sexual abuse, battered woman syndrome, and other issues related to the types of cases social workers are most likely to be called upon for testimony.

It would be difficult to overemphasize the importance and helpfulness of the American Jurisprudence Proof of Facts volumes; the information from them can prevent numerous mistakes in preparing for court. It helps tremendously to have a sense of the guidelines the court must follow in making its decisions.

DEPOSITIONS

A deposition is a type of pretrial discovery in which the opposing attorneys are attempting to learn what you will be saying in your testimony during the hearing or trial. Just as the attorneys attempt to "discover" what records you reviewed or who you have interviewed or what reports you have written, they use the deposition to try to uncover your opinions and conclusions ahead of time. In her *Witness Guide for Deposition or Court: How to Give Testimony in Any Kind of Case* (1998), Charlotte Hardwick describes the deposition as a fact-finding expedition, discovery deposition, or an evidentiary deposition for the party requesting and paying for the deposition. Put simply, Hardwick writes that "The attorney can question and cross-examine a friendly or unfriendly witness under oath outside the hearing of the judge in advance of the trial" (p. 66).

I am appreciative that Hardwick has stated a truth I wish had been made known to me earlier in my career. She writes that "If the attorney for the side paying for the deposition has unlimited funds and the rules of deposition allow, the questions could go on for days about everything from hobbies to venereal diseases one was treated for in the armed services" (p. 66). The longest deposition I ever had was five hours, but my personal life became the focus of the questioning rather than questions about the case. They asked about boyfriends and family members, substance use, and letters I had written to the editor of our local newspaper. Naturally, I am no longer surprised by anything that happens in a deposition.

The attorney should prepare you for the deposition. She will be present to stop the proceeding if necessary and go "off record," which means the court recorder will turn off the tape machine. Whether or not the questions are appropriate will be debated and then the attorney will advise you. The deposition will then go back on record.

You can be subpoenaed for a deposition and most attorneys will have a subpoena served to make sure you will be there even if you would have done so anyway. Depositions can be held in the attorneys' offices, in your office, or over the telephone. Both the opposing attorney and the attorney representing the client will be present as will a court recorder. You will be asked if you waive a copy of the transcript of your testimony given during the deposition or you can request a copy.

It is recommended that you request a copy of your testimony at deposition in order to review it before you testify at trial. The opposing attorneys will certainly review it before cross-examining you. The purpose of the deposition, in addition to discovery, is impeachment. When you get on the stand in the actual trial, the opposing attorney can use your statements in the deposition to try to see if you have changed or will contradict your testimony given during the deposition. It is perfectly acceptable to state in your deposed testimony that your assessment is ongoing. Should you become aware of any additional information prior to trial, your opinions might change. This is particularly true with the biopsychosocial assessment when new records arrive at your door the day before the trial. If something occurs after a deposition to change your opinion or conclusions, anticipate how you will explain that change on the witness stand.

THE AFFIDAVIT

Affidavits come in many forms and must be adapted to the individual case. An affidavit is basically a declaration of who you are, what you do, and what you have done or recommended on a particular case. It is formally defined as a written statement made or taken under oath before an officer of the court, notary public, or other person who has been duly authorized so to act as the attorney on your case. That person should work with you on making sure that the affidavit is comprehensive enough to provide the information needed.

The affidavit to have the court order you approved as an expert witness in a case can have a number of advantages, not the least of which is the opportunity to inform the judge about biopsychosocial assessments and to state why you are qualified to conduct one. I have provided different types of information in affidavits depending on the nature of the case. Not all affidavits are the same, nor do all require a description of the biopsychosocial assessment. If a case does call for a biopsychosocial assessment and the judge signs the court order for you to conduct the assessment, she is basically saying that you are competent to do the work and report your findings to the court. Example 1 is a sample affidavit that thoroughly informs the court on exactly what is going to take place. It also covers time required, expenses, and fees; however, this information may not always be required in the affidavit. Many affidavits are shorter than this sample, but language in this affidavit can be helpful in preparing one of your own. Example 2 is a sample of a basic, one-page affidavit.

The American Jurisprudence Proof of Facts volumes mentioned earlier in this chapter give samples of affidavits. Attorneys will generally request one if needed for the case. You will rarely have to make that decision yourself. I have offered to do an affidavit in certain cases. For example, in lieu of going to court and when agreed upon with the attorney, I have submitted affidavits to the court that are a detailed accounting of my intervention with a client and my conclusions.

It is also permissible to testify that you have read the affidavit of another witness as part of your review of documents in a case. If the lawyer has the sworn statement of a doctor, neighbor, teacher, etc., and you reviewed that statement in preparing your own evaluation, you can testify that you have seen that affidavit and relied upon the information contained therein.

EXAMPLE 1. Sample of Affidavit for Biopsychosocial Assessment

The following would appear under your letterhead:

AFFIDAVIT

1. I am a licensed clinical social worker and (whatever title you may hold) in (town, state). I have received certification and licensing from the following institutions:
   (List licensing boards, certifying boards, and numbers.)

2. I received my BA degree from (school) in (year), and a master's degree in Social Work from (school) in (year). I received my doctorate in Social Work from (school) in (year). I completed social work internships at (list internships and years).

3. I hold memberships in the following organizations:
   (List organizations and include positions of present or past president. Also list board chairmanships.)

4. I have been appointed by:
   (List appointments even if it is a single appointment.)

5. I have delivered speeches and seminars in the following areas:
   (List speeches and seminars.)

6. I have worked in a variety of social work settings:
   (List settings and years. You may describe some detail of these positions, but keep it fairly brief.)

7. I am often asked to explain my findings to the court, and I have testified as an expert on numerous occasions. (If your court experience is different, state what it has been in this first sentence. If it is your first time, state simply that you have been asked to explain your findings in the case.) A biopsychosocial assessment is conducted in order to determine if there are any factors that would explain how the client has come to be in his current situation. These factors may be social, emotional, medical, or intellectual. The assessment includes a review of all documents that can be obtained that relate to the client's life (school, medical, social services, juvenile, military, etc.). Interviews are conducted with persons significant in the client's life, and other experts are consulted in order to compare findings and confirm your own opinions. In some cases, your opinion may vary from those of other experts and this can lead to new information. Research and other literature that relates to the issues in the case are reviewed and considered. This assessment differs from a psychiatric evaluation or psychological assessment in that it typically requires between 100 and 200 hours. It is more comprehensive and greater in scope than the psychiatric or psychological evaluation. It is routine for doctors to request biopsychosocial assessments from trained social workers.

8. The assessment typically includes:

   A. *At least two sources for all facts uncovered from:*

      (1) Interviews with family members (as many as can be located), neighbors, friends, clergy, teachers, coworkers, and any other significant individuals who had contact with the client.

(2) A review of records (medical, school, dental, social services, court documents, police records, military, mental health, institutional, etc.).

(3) An assessment of poverty and deprivation (re: client and family) and assessment of the availability of food, money, shelter, mental health care, medical care, special education, social support, nurturance, attachment, stigmatization; impact of unmet needs on mental health care, medical care, special education, social support, nurturance, attachment, stigmatization; and impact of unmet needs on development.

(4) An exploration of all areas of competence including personal and social strengths (e.g., whatever the client does well).

(5) An exploration of all major losses (e.g., relationships, changing homes/ neighborhoods, schools, divorces, deaths, accidents, suicides) and responses to loss (coping skills).

(6) An exploration of all traumas, extraordinary stressors (e.g., victimization, serious illnesses, exposure to disaster, community violence, parental mental illness or substance abuse) and how the client typically responds to above.

(7) Interviews with other experts who have evaluated the client in addition to a review of their records.

B. *Topics to be covered in assessment:*

(1) Prenatal and birth history of all family members
(2) Residential history, community and its institutions, cultural makeup
(3) Early child development
(4) School-age development
(5) Adolescent development
(6) Adult history
(7) Topics to cover in the social history:

- Entire family composition/changes from birth through present noting all deaths, broken relationships, family dynamics, client's role in the family.
- Significant social network composition: changes from birth through present noting all deaths, broken relationships, positive and negative aspects of networks.
- Residential history noting all transitions and characteristics of the neighborhoods; institutional placements and characteristics of the institutions.
- Early child development: prenatal (e.g., mother's physical and emotional status during pregnancy), perinatal, infancy, preschool. Note all developmental milestones, delays, deviations from normalcy; include physical, intellectual, biopsychosocial.
- School-age development: physical, intellectual, biopsychosocial characteristics; academic achievement relative to potential; social adjustment at home, school, neighborhood.
- Adolescent development: physical, intellectual, biopsychosocial characteristics; academic achievement relative to potential; social adjustment at home, school, neighborhood, workplace; sexual development and activity; alcohol/drug use.

- Adult history: educational attainment, work history, religious practices, relational history (e.g., marriage, children), sexual functioning, recreational interests, health/mental health status, personality.
- Broader ecosystem issues, such as subcultural issues, social norms of the community in which the client lived, public policy issues that directly affected the client's life.

C. *Genograms, charts, and other visual aids to assist in explaining client's behavior:*

Biopsychosocial assessments typically require between 100 and 200 hours depending on the nature of the case (the number of hours will vary depending on your case and your work setting) and distance that must be traveled for interviews.

Fees range between $50 and $120 an hour depending on travel, interviews, and court testimony. The fee is also affected by the amount of standard fees charged in a particular region of the country.

If a comprehensive investigation has been conducted, hours may vary depending on the amount of information obtained. Time and fee estimates fall within the standard amount charged among professional social workers performing these duties. Extraneous expenses are accommodations, transportation, etc.

_____

(signature)

Sworn before me _____

on this day _____

My Commission Expires _____

EXAMPLE 2. One-Page Affidavit

AFFIDAVIT

I, Janet Vogelsang, MSW, LISW, declare:

A. That I am a licensed independent social worker in the state of South Carolina and that I have a private practice in Greenville, South Carolina.

B. That John Jones was referred to me on August 21, 1995, for an assessment of his parental skills. He was seen on five occasions, and on three of those occasions he was seen with his two sons.

C. That I visited the home of John Jones and saw the children in the home with their father.

D. That I have run a check with the South Carolina Law Enforcement Division (SLED) and the child abuse registry and find no prior arrests or reports of abuse or violence.

E. That John Jones appears to have exceptional parenting skills and that his children appear to be in no danger in his care.

F. That unsupervised weekend visitations would be appropriate in this case.

_____

(signature)

Sworn before me _____

on this day _____

My Commission Expires _____

DISCOVERY

To understand discovery, it is important to first consider the issue of attorney work product. Poynter (1987) describes the meaning of work product, which should be limited to the attorney's notes on a case. Literally, the attorney work product is the work notes produced by the attorney in preparing a case. If an attorney is strategizing a case and wants to list the positives and negatives of her case, she can do so without worrying that the opposing counsel will have a right to "discover" those notes and use the negative aspects of the case to his own advantage.

Many attorneys will discuss a case with you in the process of learning more about the client. Because there is no report involved and because the comments are oral, the attorney's notes are not subject to discovery. The rules change once you move from the consulting role into the witness role (Poynter, 1987). As a witness, the opposing side has a right to see whatever you have in your file. As a social worker, not an attorney, I am often confused by what is discoverable and what is not. Poynter states that "information communicated by the client-attorney to the expert witness may be privileged if the information is necessary for the expert to accomplish his or her job. If your client-attorney steers your investigation in the proper direction, the communication may not be discoverable" (p. 69).

The issue of discoverability is important to social workers because of the biopsychosocial assessment. Because we review records, research, studies, literature, books, correspondence, etc., those items may be discoverable by the other side. I always list the records I reviewed and am prepared to produce them if requested.

Always talk to the attorney on your case about discovery. Ask about his interpretation of discovery rules and if there are any exceptions. If your file contains negative information about a client, you will have to factor it into your overview of the client and be prepared to answer questions about such notes on the witness stand. Perfect clients do not exist, and frankly I believe jurors can see right through any effort to show someone in too perfect a light. The biopsychosocial assessment looks at strengths and weaknesses. If your file contains something believed by the attorney to be damaging to his client, it is his duty to protect his client and to decide whether to retain you.

LEGAL DEFINITIONS

The following glossary contains the most frequently used legal terms I have encountered throughout many court cases. They were taken from *Law Dictionary,* Third Edition, by Steven H. Gifis (1991). The dictionary has over 3,000 legal terms explained in helpful detail with references. The referenced citations are explained by the author but I have paraphrased the definitions to simplify what social workers need to know. It is well worth owning a copy of this dictionary so that if you should need further cites for a certain legal term, you can find them easily.

adjudication: A formal judgment by the court; a court order that is a pronouncement of the court's decision.

admissibility: Addresses whether the evidence in question can be admitted or must be excluded according to the rules of evidence.

affidavit: A written statement of facts sworn before a notary public or an officer of the court.

appeal: A request before a higher court to have arguments heard to review and reverse the lower court's decision.

arguments: Statements made to the court in an effort to reason each party's positions on a legal matter.

arraignment: An initial criminal procedure in which a defendant is charged with the offense for which he stands accused.

attorney-client privilege: Refers to the confidential communications between an attorney and a client. Information shared with an attorney cannot be disclosed without client consention

bailiff: A court attendant entrusted with keeping order in the courtroom as well as being in charge of the jury.

character witness: A lay witness who testifies about his or her personal knowledge of the character and reputation of another person.

closing statement: A statement made by the attorney at the end of the case that summarizes the proceedings.

competent: Capable of acting reasonably and the capacity to understand certain things.

complaint: The initial pleading by a plaintiff. A complaint needs only to demonstrate a short statement of the claim.

contempt of court: The obstruction of court procedure in a manner that disrespects or affects the dignity of the court.

court clerk: An officer of the court who maintains records and enters judgments.

court order: A formally written judgment from the court that directs some matter addressed in the proceeding.

court reporter: The individual who records the testimony and other proceedings in the court or in depositions.

cross-examination: Questions asked of a witness by the opposing attorney which address statements made by the witness during direct examination.

custody of children: The legal control of a minor child given to a parent or guardian in a divorce, abuse, or other situation in which the placement of the child is in question.

defendant: An individual who must account for a wrong brought against him or her by the plaintiff.

defense attorney: The lawyer who acts on behalf of the individual who has been named the defendant.

demonstrations (demonstrative evidence): An object that the jury can touch, examine, or observe that has been presented as hard evidence to the jury.

deposition: Oral testimony taken prior to the trial by the opposing attorney; an attempt by the opposing attorney to discover what the witness will say.

direct examination: The initial interrogation of a witness by the party calling the witness to testify.

directed verdict: A verdict given by the court in a jury trial. This may occur when the judge believes that the facts in concert with the law can only result in a certain verdict.

discovery: A procedure that occurs before a trial in which one party obtains information which is held by the other party.

docket: The court calendar; A case placed on the docket by the court clerk will have a docket number.

due process: A guarantee that every person will have access to a fair trial. The basis for due process is the Fifth Amendment to the Constitution which states that no one should be deprived of life, liberty, or property without due process of law.

error: A mistake made in the course of a legal proceeding which could lead to a change in or reversal of a judgment.

exclusionary rules: A rule of law based on a constitutional provision that certain evidence, which might otherwise be admissible, cannot be used if it resulted from an illegal police search or seizure.

exhibit: An item, such as a gun or a piece of clothing, which is presented as real evidence before the court.

ex parte: Usually refers to a motion made by one party only. In an ex parte judicial hearing, only one party is represented without challenge by an adverse party.

expert witness: A witness whose knowledge is not usually held by the average individual and whose testimony is based on special knowledge of a subject.

foreman (foreperson): The juror chosen to preside over the jury and who is seated in the first position in the jury box. It is the duty of the foreperson to communicate between the jury and the court.

forensic: As it applies to the courts, e.g., one can have special knowledge in a field of practice such as clinical social work and when the expertise is presented in court, it becomes forensic.

grand jury: A jury of inquiry drawn for the purpose of investigating accusations in criminal cases and determining if there is probable cause that a crime was committed and whether to go forth with a trial. This procedure concludes with a bill of indictment when the grand jury decides that it has sufficient evidence that a crime has been committed.

guardian: One who is appointed by the court to protect and manage the affairs of a minor or an individual found to be incompetent.

habeas corpus: A Latin term meaning "You have the body." A writ of habeas corpus is used in federal courts to test whether due process of law has been conducted in a state criminal proceeding. It is also used to test the legality of confinement of a defendant in a criminal matter.

harmless error: An error that has occurred in a legal proceeding but which is not prejudicial enough to affect the appellant's rights and cause the court to overturn or modify a lower court decision.

hearing: A court proceeding in which evidence is presented for the purpose of adjudication or investigation.

hearsay rule: Evidence given in testimony that could be construed as rumor rather than personal knowledge of a matter by the witness who is testifying.

hostile witness: A witness who can be cross-examined by the party who called him to the stand because of his hostility toward the opposing party.

hypothetical question: A set of circumstances that assumes certain facts, some of which may be already proven, and is stated in such a way that it calls upon the expert witness to give an opinion based on those circumstances as they are presented, whether or not they are totally factual.

impeach: To attack the credibility of a witness through documentation or the testimony of another witness. Information given in a deposition prior to trial can be used to impeach a witness as well as official statements made to law officers.

incompetency: The lack of capacity to perform certain duties and responsibilities; or a physical or mental impairment such that one cannot appreciate the nature of one's own actions.

indictment: An accusation presented in writing by a grand jury which has determined that there is sufficient evidence to accuse an individual of a crime.

in loco parentis: A Latin term that means "in place of the parent." Refers to a person who, without a legal proceeding such as adoption, acts as a lawful parent in terms of the duties and responsibilities he or she assumes on behalf of a minor.

insanity: The degree to which a mentally impaired individual can be held legally responsible for his or her actions whether criminal or financial.

instruction: A direction, usually lengthy, given by the judge to the jury regarding the law that is applicable to the facts of the case. This information is given before the jury adjourns to deliberate.

interrogatories: Formally written questions presented before trial to the opposing side that seek written replies. This tool is used as a form of discovery.

judgment: The final decision or determination by the judge in a legal matter such as a lawsuit.

jurisdiction: The power to make decisions which are legally binding over a person or property.

jury: A number of people selected according to the law and whose duty it is to examine certain facts and to decide upon the truth based on the evidence presented to them.

lay witness: A witness who is not before the court as an expert giving an opinion, but one who testifies to perceptions or helps clarify a fact.

leading question: A question that suggests an answer or prompts the witness toward a certain answer.

malpractice: A purposeful or careless performance in conducting professional duties.

material witness: A witness who can be held against his or her will to guarantee presence at the trial; one whose testimony is such that the legal matter may not be resolved without this testimony.

Miranda Rule: This rule allows a person to have an attorney and to remain silent before any questioning by law enforcement.

M'naghton Rule: A rule in which criminal responsibility can be tested exclusive of insanity. The rule states that the individual was not responsible if behavior was the result of a mental disease or if the individual did not know right from wrong.

motion: A request made formally to the judge in reference to a pending action; a motion may also be made concerning a point of law.

negligence: Failure to do something an ordinary person in an ordinary situation would deem reasonable to do.

objection: The act of asserting that a legal matter is being improperly or illegally conducted and should be ruled upon by the court; usually used by an opposing attorney during examination of a witness, to point out to the judge a question or answer believed to be improperly asked or answered.

opening statement: The statement given to the jury by attorneys representing both sides and laying out their opposing theories on the matter being brought before the court.

overrule: Denial of a motion made to the court or denial of an objection, e.g., "objection overruled." If the judge agrees with the objection he or she will sustain it. If the judge disagrees, it will be overruled.

plaintiff: The person who brings the complaint before the court or who sues.

plea bargaining: A process in which the defendant and the prosecutor agree to disposition of the case satisfactory to both sides. A plea bargain usually results in the defendant agreeing to a lesser charge in order to receive a lighter sentence than if tried for several more serious charges.

pleadings: Legal statements of the facts for which a plaintiff has brought an action. The defendant's pleadings are a legal statement outlining the grounds for his defense.

preponderance of the evidence: In civil actions, the weight of the credible that is more convincing than the evidence presented by the opposing side.

pro bono: Latin phrase that describes a case taken by an attorney who has agreed not to accept compensation.

prosecutor: Typically the title given to the attorney who brings a case to trial and who represents the people. The lawyer who works for the state and, based upon the evidence, works to bring the accused to trial and tries the case.

protective custody: The protection of an individual through confinement by the state in order to prevent harm to that person.

public defender: The attorney hired by the state to defend the accused in a criminal court.

reasonable doubt: The state of mind of the jury which requires a certain degree of certainty in order to find a defendant guilty. If the jury cannot find the defendant guilty beyond a reasonable doubt, then the accused is entitled to acquittal.

rebuttal: The stage of a trial when evidence may be presented refuting what has been previously stated.

restraining order: An order that keeps a legal matter as it is, or maintains the status quo until a hearing can be held. A restraining order can be granted without notice or a hearing.

search warrant: An order that brings a person or a thing before the court. The search warrant gives permission to law enforcement to find the person or thing specified in the order.

sequester: The separation of the jury or the witnesses in a legal proceeding as a way of monitoring or preventing improper conduct.

statute of limitations: The limit on a time period in which a legal matter may be taken to court.

subpoena: A process by which a formally written document is delivered that orders a person to appear in court or before a magistrate.

subpoena duces tecum: A process by a formally written document in which a witness is required to bring to court documents and records related to a legal matter.

summons: A process in which a law enforcement officer is required to notify an individual in a legal action to appear before the court.

transcript: The document taken, copied, and certified by a court recorder of a court proceeding or deposition.

trial: A legal proceeding in which the parties to a particular issue present evidence and facts in order to have the court make a decision to the truth of the matter.

trier of fact: Those in a legal proceeding who find the facts. The judge may be the trier of fact and the trier of law; the jury is more typically the trier of fact.

venue: The city, county, or other place in which a court with jurisdiction may hold a legal proceeding.

verdict: The formal finding or decision by a jury or a judge and one that has been accepted by the court.

voir dire: The examination of potential jurors by attorneys to assess whether they qualify to serve on the jury.

work product: Documents held by or produced by an attorney in the course of case preparation and which are not subject to discovery by the opposing attorney.

THE COURT SYSTEM AND DEFINITIONS: SUMMARY

1. Familiarize yourself with court systems in your community, region, jurisdiction, and state.
2. Read the state and federal rules of evidence especially as they apply to expertise and hearsay.
3. Discover the American Jurisprudence Proof of Facts volumes in a law library, and review the issues important to the court when hearing your particular type of case.
4. Ask the lawyer on your case to familiarize you with affidavits, depositions, discovery, and other legal language and situations related to your case.
5. Obtain a good law dictionary for legal definitions and terms.

Chapter 2

The Biopsychosocial Assessment
As Expertise

The subject of the biopsychosocial assessment in practice and for use in the courts could also stand alone as a book. For the purposes of testifying in court, it is crucial to have a clear understanding of how the assessment is closely connected to thorough and informative testimony that is not constantly diminished by objections to hearsay. The building blocks of the assessment can make you an excellent presenter of your findings to the judge and the jury.

Over the years, I have watched clinical social workers and other professionals struggle to justify their expertise in certain areas. They are disappointed if they are not qualified as experts, but even after successful qualification they lament being limited to a focus so narrow as to prevent them from saying anything helpful to the court.

You will notice in this book that information which might be helpful to the jury or to the court is frequently mentioned. Why? in establishing expertise in conducting biopsychosocial assessments, the clinical social work expert is stating that one of the purposes of the biopsychosocial assessment is to educate not only the client or the client's family, but to provide information to organizations or groups who might request it, such as the courts. In an agency or private practice setting, the information might be used in educating the client or family and then in forming a treatment plan. When providing information discovered in the biopsychosocial assessment to the court, it is important to remember that the information is going to be used to help the judge or jury make an informed decision regarding the client or the situation.

On the witness stand you want to be able to describe the biopsychosocial assessment to the jury. The assessment is the tool you use to evaluate the client (yours, the attorney's, the court's, or all three), and to form your conclusions and opinions. You must be able to define the biopsychosocial assessment in a way that is clear and understandable.

Why does the clinical social worker go to court and try to be qualified as an expert in everything from soup to nuts? It is because we have careers that dictate the wearing of many hats in our day-to-day functioning. But it does not work in the courtroom. We come across as vague, uncertain, and confused about who we are and what we do. We have all sat at professional board meetings agonizing over how to clarify our field.

For most of our day-to-day clients, we are mother, father, sister, brother, therapist, advocate, teacher, spiritual advisor, etc. We work in offices, in the field, overseas, in prisons, in hospitals, and in private settings. We provide most of the mental health services in America and are reimbursed by insurance companies. Twelve of our own advised on and contributed to the *Diagnostic and Statistical Manual*, Fourth Edition, the psychiatric bible (APA, 1994). Axis IV of the *Diagnostic and Statistical Manual* includes a category for biopsychosocial stressors. Not only is there a specific category gory for biopsychosocial stressors, but the impact of those stressors considered is placing diagnoses on the other four axes (if you are dealing with a competent and caring psychiatrist or psychologist, that is). Social work research, study, and treatment of family systems and environmental stressors as well as the inclusion of medical and psychological factors in our assessments have increased our influence in the psychiatric community and resulted in greater care in the way clients are diagnosed.

Who deals with biopsychosocial stressors in a more intimate manner than the clinical social worker? No one. Do psychiatrists and psychologists typically visit the homes, neighborhoods, and communities of their clients? Do they typically call teachers, neighbors, friends, ministers, and others into their offices or do they visit them on site? Do they maintain lists of resources for their clients or research new resources? Do they arrange for resources that match the needs of their clients? Do they typically design visual aids to educate their clients in a language the client can understand? Do they read hundreds of pages of records from the past or even believe that those records are important? Do they obtain in-depth family histories going back at least three generations? Do they search for documents that would validate certain experiences reported by the client? Do they look for consistency in those volumes of information? Do they typically consult with other experts outside their fields or their offices?

As clinical social workers we have the most intensely personal and comprehensive understanding of our clients. Our perspective is more valued, respected, and requested than ever before in our professional history.

Some other professionals may do one or two of the tasks mentioned above, and certainly there are clinical social workers who get out of the habit of using the biopsychosocial assessment. The use of the biopsychosocial assessment will not only make you an excellent witness in court, it will also improve your skills in the practice of your profession and improve the services to your client.

RELEARNING THE BIOPSYCHOSOCIAL ASSESSMENT

Does one really come out of graduate school with a firm grasp on the value of the biopsychosocial assessment? Does the new social worker, armed with an academic understanding of the assessment and field placements for practice, run up against the hard reality of everyday practice and slowly shed crucial elements of the assessment in an effort to meet time demands, money demands, and the demands of heavy caseloads?

According to Brill and Taler (1990), great difficulty is experienced by teachers of social work in training their students to make biopsychosocial assessments and to present them coherently. Are the colleges of social work at fault? Efforts to locate teaching materials and texts on the subject left me aware of the need for greater emphasis in this area. Use of the biopsychosocial assessment in the courts has made me a better practitioner with private clients because the assessment, when used properly, demands attention to detail that is too often easily overlooked.

The presentation on the biopsychosocial assessment by Brill and Taler, while superior in the elements of the assessment that it covers, limits itself to data collection concerning interviews only. While the spiral model introduced by these talented and thoughtful social workers is well worth reviewing, the model ignores records, other evaluations, other professional opinions and assessments, testing, and medical concerns. The biopsychosocial assessment does not need to be a medical model nor should it ignore medical issues. If one were to approach the witness stand having conducted a biopsychosocial assessment based on the Brill and Taler spiral model of interviewing, one would be sadly left at the mercy of the opposing attorney and the cross-examination.

Definition of the Biopsychosocial Assessment

The biopsychosocial assessment is a social work tool that is used to explain human behavior. It is a broad and comprehensive process that includes interviews with the client and others who are important to the client; the review of documents that have been generated about the client and others who are important to the client; a search for studies, journal articles, or other publications that address issues related to those of the client; consultation with other experts; and the creation of visual aids, when appropriate, to help explain the information gathered. In a private or agency setting, this information is used to educate and form treatment plans or to provide resources. In public settings such as the court, the biopsychosocial assessment is used to provide information that would assist the judge and jury in making their decisions. It is designed to provide as many sources of information as possible and to ensure consistency of information. Be aware that there are now those professionals and nonprofessionals who conduct "social histories," which they claim are the same as biopsychosocial assessments. We have an obligation to make attorneys and the court aware of the difference, and to educate them as to why a true biopsychosocial assessment is conducted by a trained clinical social worker. Psychiatrists and psychologists will take the witness stand and claim to have done a biopsychosocial assessment or "family background" or "social history" assessment in a one-hour interview. This is impossible! They are not trained to do biopsychosocial assessments nor can they be done in an hour or less.

Most distressing of all are social workers in certain settings who believe that a three-page, fill-in-the-blank form required by their agency or hospital is an adequate social work assessment. There are even settings where the social worker is filling out the family background form without ever interviewing the client. Quite a feat! These talented professionals are allowing others without their knowledge or training to dictate their roles and reduce their effectiveness on behalf of the client. While it is true that managing large caseloads can be prohibitive in terms of conducting a comprehensive assessment on each and every client or patient, strategic planning can allow for much more information than might be obtained otherwise.

When you graduate from a college of social work, you have education and training in conducting biopsychosocial assessments. You have experience from your field placement or internship, and as you practice, you gain new skills and knowledge about the importance of this social work tool. You also run up against enormous caseloads, too few investigators, staffing and budget problems, and lack of time. Arguably, private practitioners have greater flexibility regarding time spent on an assessment. The truth is that more information is always out there and, for various reasons, we will never get all of it. Many times I have found myself in the position of needing to criticize a one- or two-page "social work assessment" from an agency or institution. It is not pleasant to have to show why a social work colleague's assessment was not proper or complete. It is especially disconcerting to have to do it on the witness stand. But when my assessment includes numerous hours interviewing people who know the client, visiting the communities of the client, interviewing other experts involved with the client, reading hundreds of pages of documents on the client and his family, and reviewing literature that relates to my client, then I can testify that a comprehensive biopsychosocial assessment has been conducted. It is then left to the judge and the jury to decide which assessment helps them the most. You can guess which assessment will carry the most weight. It is most uncomfortable to be in a legal situation in which the inadequacies of another social worker's assessment must be addressed.

Qualifying As an Expert in Conducting Biopsychosocial Assessments

Although a section is included in this book on testifying about the biopsychosocial assessment in the context of qualifying as an expert witness, the following sample questions might be asked about the biopsychosocial assessment.

Direct Examination Questions

> **Q.** Ms. Vogelsang, as a social worker, do you have any specialty areas or areas where you have special knowledge or expertise?
> **A.** Yes. My specialties are child welfare, trauma, family systems, and conducting biopsychosocial assessments both in my practice and for the courts.
> **Q.** What is a biopsychosocial assessment?
> **A.** The biopsychosocial assessment is a social work tool that is used to explain or help understand human behavior. It consists of interviews, review of records, consulting with other experts, research and literature reviews, and depending on the circumstances for which it will be used, visual aids. With this assessment, an attempt is made to have at least two or more sources of information before drawing any conclusions or opinions. The assessment seeks to find consistency in the information provided as

well as provide an understanding of the client's behavior and circumstances.

Q. And is it standard for social workers to use this method of assessment in agencies, hospitals, and other settings?

A. Yes.

Q. If I were to ask a social worker in California or New York to do this assessment, would they be doing pretty much the same thing?

A. Depending on the setting and circumstances, yes.

Cross-Examination Questions

Q. Ms. Vogelsang, isn't this biopsychosocial assessment just a tool for making excuses for bad behavior?

A. The assessment is definitely not an excuse for any type of behavior. It is used to explain certain behaviors and circumstances and how family history, environment, and life experiences have played roles in those behaviors. It will hopefully shed light on the current circumstance and help the court to gain additional understanding of the present situation.

CASE EXAMPLE AND TESTIMONY USING THE BIOPSYCHOSOCIAL ASSESSMENT

This example is a case in which the young client had grown up in a violent and drug-ridden neighborhood. In order to find a second source of information to substantiate the information obtained in interviews with the client and his family members, an investigator was asked to take me to the neighborhood where the young man had spent all of his childhood years. A Saturday morning was chosen for this trip, and the grid of streets selected proved to be a wealth of visual information. Drug dealers were already working their corners, drunks were passed out in doorways, prostitutes were still out strolling the streets, and children were out and about among the vandalized buildings and trash-strewn streets of an area that looked like a war zone. We rode up and down the streets, outlining the number of blocks and naming the streets that bordered this community.

As requested, the investigator then went to the local police department and asked for a sampling of the crime statistics for the years during which the client claimed to have witnessed numerous neighborhood crimes. The client had also revealed the story of his introduction to drugs by his father, his recruitment into drug selling by an older dealer, and his own use of drugs beginning at age eleven. The investigator gave the police department the border streets we had identified and asked for the crime statistics covering that area during the years we wanted to examine. As suspected, the crime statistics accurately portrayed the information the client, his family, and his neighbors had described. Combined with my personal observations of the community and a chart of the crime statistics, the information from the interviews could be credibly supported. The entire process required only a couple of hours on my part. Actually, with one phone call or a quick letter, I could have easily obtained the crime statistics myself.

Direct Examination Questions

> **Q.** Ms. Vogelsang, you stated that you learned in your interviews that the Holmes Community was a drug-ridden, violent neighborhood. How do you know that this is the case?
>
> **A.** I visited the community, and drove up and down the streets.
>
> **Q.** And could you describe for the courts what you saw?
>
> **A.** Yes. I observed glass-strewn streets, broken windows in houses and buildings, drug dealing on street corners, prostitution, and drunks passed out in doorways.
>
> **Q.** Ms. Vogelsang, how do you know that all of that was going on when Mr. Smith lived in that neighborhood?

A. I requested police statistics for the years that he lived there and the years he believes he witnessed the deaths I have mentioned earlier.

Q. Do you have a chart that demonstrates those statistics?

A. Yes.

Q. Was the information on your chart taken directly from the statistics you obtained from the police department?

A. Yes.

Q. And do you have the original copies of the statistics from the police department with you?

A. Yes.

Now take a look at direct testimony and cross-examination based on family and client interviews only.

Direct Testimony from Interviews Only

Q. Ms. Vogelsang, who did you interview about the neighborhood where Mr. Smith grew up?

A. Mr. Smith, his mother, two of his brothers, and his minister.

Q. And what did you learn from those interviews?

A. That there were a lot of drugs and drug dealers around, that robberies were common, and that Mr. Smith saw a lot of violence including people getting shot and stabbed.

Cross-Examination Testimony from Interviews Only

Q. Ms. Vogelsang, did you conduct those interviews in person or by telephone?

A. I saw Mr. Smith in person and the rest were by telephone.

Q. Wouldn't Mr. Smith and his family, and even his minister, want to tell you things that would help him out of this jam?

A. I have been a social worker for a long time and I have the background, training, and experience to do these interviews.

Q. Yes, but Ms. Vogelsang, are you telling us that you can tell if someone is lying or not?

A. No, but I rely on my experience in interviewing.

Q. So you believe everything you are told by someone you saw in your office one time, and all the rest you interviewed by telephone?

A. No, but I think I have skills to form these opinions.

Q. Ms. Vogelsang, you don't really know anything about that neighborhood except what the family told you, now do you?

A. No.

You can clearly see how easily the cross-examiner has dismantled your observations and cast doubt on your credibility.

In the first example, which is the correct way to use the biopsychosocial assessment to prepare for court testimony, the chart mentioned was an enlargement of the neighborhood crime statistics covering about five years. It showed a breakdown of murders, armed robberies, breaking and entering, drug arrests, prostitution, assaults, and one or two other categories. It confirmed the information obtained in interviews, and showed that the client had told the truth about his neighborhood and the violence he witnessed on a daily basis.

This small sampling of testimony illustrates that, with the interviews and records, the usefulness of the biopsychosocial assessment and its consistent information can be demonstrated to the court. Information from the interviews, one visit to the community, and the police statistics gathered by the investigator verified that the client had in fact grown up in the violent environment he had described. I have heard many expert witnesses get very huffy and insulted when the court does not take their word for it. You must be able to support your findings.

With proper planning, time management, and the efficient use of resources such as family members and investigators, the clinical social worker can initiate much of the information needed for the biopsychosocial assessment by phone. Some agencies and institutions dictate what the clinical social worker can and cannot do. A job description often limits the scope of the clinical social worker's role. In that case, the clinical social worker must acknowledge to the court that the assessments were limited by the constraints of the settings. A legal case is a major and often life-altering event for a client. It must be addressed with a high degree of thoroughness.

BIOPSYCHOSOCIAL ASSESSMENT QUESTIONNAIRES

Family background questionnaires found in most agencies and institutions are generally not detailed enough either for good, solid treatment planning or for the courts. Good assessment questions can be found both in and out of social work settings, and collecting a file of published and unpublished assessment questions can be most helpful. Resisting the impulse to form premature hypotheses (Lukas, 1993) is one of the best reasons for a thorough assessment. Although Lukas has written on the assessment phase for mental health settings, her detailed questionnaires are most useful in gathering information in the beginning stages of the biopsychosocial assessment for use in the courtroom.

The intake questionnaire designed by psychologist Arnold Lazarus is one of the most thorough and comprehensive I have found. Although it is typically used in a private setting, this questionnaire can be especially productive when seeking the kind of detail one might need when legal matters are involved. In *The Practice of Multimodal Therapy,* Lazarus (1989) outlines the kinds of questions one must ask to plan treatment on several levels of functioning. Because the biopsychosocial assessment examines the individual from a number of different perspectives, the broad coverage of the multimodal questionnaire is particularly helpful.

One of the most exciting and compelling assessment tools origi-
nated by our profession is the person-in-environment (PIE) system
developed by Karls and Wandrei (1994). As they have noted in this
classification system of social functioning problems, social workers have for too long had to rely on the *Diagnostic and Statistical
Manual of Mental Disorders* (DSM-IV). The PIE system has been
published (NASW Press) and is an excellent resource for assessment. I am hesitant to make reference to the system in court testimony simply because it is new, and an attorney who is on his toes
will undoubtedly make an issue of that newness. It is gratifying,
however, that Karls and Wandrei have pioneered this amazing system and as it evolves over time, future social workers will have an
invaluable tool to use in conducting their assessments and offering
their opinions in court. Just as psychiatrists and psychologists rely
on the DSM-IV in the courtroom, we will have not only the DSM
ad infinitum but also our own system of the classification of social
functioning.

It is important that we begin now to familiarize ourselves with the
PIE system for use in our assessments. The manual that accompanies the person-in-environment system of classification (Karls and
Wandrei, 1994) also outlines the social and environmental areas
into which one must dig conscientiously when conducting the
biopsychosocial assessment. The manual also has a severity, dura-
tion, and coping index to assist in the assessment.

Depending on the information you are receiving, you often need
to turn to other sources for appropriate questions to ask. For example, suppose you learn that the client has a history of attention deficit disorder. Do you know enough about the disorder to ask the
right questions? In this case, I would turn to the work of Dr. Edna
Copeland (Copeland and Love, 1995), who has developed numerous questionnaires to assess the family background and developmental history of her clients.

Using the biopsychosocial assessment as a framework for conducting interviews, reviewing records, consulting with other experts and professionals, and reviewing research and literature is
essential to preparing for court testimony. This social work tool is
the backbone of our profession.

THE BIOPSYCHOSOCIAL ASSESSMENT: SUMMARY

1. Know how to define the biopsychosocial assessment.
2. Be prepared to explain your training and experience in conducting biopsychosocial assessments.
3. Use the biopsychosocial assessment framework for preparing your court testimony.
   - Interviews
   - Records and other documentation
   - Consultation with other experts
   - Research and literature
   - Visual aids
4. Be prepared to defend the biopsychosocial assessment as your area of expertise.
5. Be prepared to diplomatically and respectfully explain why your expertise in conducting biopsychosocial assessments is different from a "social history" conducted by either a non-social worker or a trained social worker who has complied with the minimal requirements of his or her agency or other setting.
6. If you have expertise in other areas, be prepared to discuss that expertise on the witness stand and combine it with expertise in conducting biopsychosocial assessments.

Chapter 3

Working with the Lawyer on Your Case

A good lawyer calls you weeks or even months in advance of the court date. A good lawyer is one who, knowing of your involvement with the client, calls upon you from the very beginning.

This ideal lawyer would not be hung up on directing every aspect of the case. She would respect the client and the expertise of the clinical social worker. She would get to know her client and the client's family. She would visit the client's home and neighborhood at least once. She would never ask you to say something you cannot substantiate, but would focus on what you can say. She would stay in contact with you as you work with the client and meet with you periodically to stay current on how the client is doing. She would insist on talking to you at regular intervals.

Wake up! This ideal scenario is not going to happen. Due to situations beyond our control, we sometimes must go to court whether or not we are prepared by the attorney. But in most situations we have some options. If an attorney calls and asks you to do a biopsychosocial assessment for a criminal case that begins in one week, say no! Yes, lawyers can be charming, flattering, convincing, guilt inducing, persistent, and all the other things they call upon in order to win in court. They can make you think that the outcome of the case rests on your shoulders (it does not) or that you are their star witness (not likely). They might become angry and try to intimidate you when you say no. You must keep in mind that you can do a lot of damage to the individual you have assessed by testifying from an incomplete biopsychosocial assessment; a thorough assessment can take weeks or even months. You are setting yourself up by agreeing to testify on short notice, unless of course you are being asked to speak about a specialty area such as sexual abuse and not specifically about the client. The following is an example of such testimony.

EXAMPLE OF TESTIMONY
WITHOUT REFERENCE TO THE CLIENT

Q. Ms. Vogelsang, you have been qualified as an expert in the area of the sexual abuse of children. About how many cases have you assessed over the course of your professional career?

A. Hundreds.

Q. Have you had any special training or certifications in this area?

A. Yes, I have.

Q. And do other professionals in your community refer clients to you who have been sexually abused?

A. Yes, they do.

Q. And in your private practice do you assess and treat children, adolescents, and adults who have been victims of sexual abuse?

A. Yes, I do.

Q. What do most professionals like yourself mean when they use the words "sexual abuse?" What are they talking about?

A. (At this point, one would describe the definition of sexual abuse without ever mentioning the client.)

Q. Ms. Vogelsang, what kind of symptoms do you most often observe in children who have been sexually abused?

A. (Again, in describing the symptoms, one is careful not to mention the client.)

Q. And Ms. Vogelsang, what is the impact most likely to be seen in children who have been sexually abused?

A. (Be careful. It becomes difficult, especially if the child or the family is in the courtroom, to refrain from mentioning this specific case.)

Q. Do parents who sexually abuse their children have any particular traits in common?

A. (Be doubly careful. The attorney representing the alleged perpetrator is waiting for you to make a mistake. She is watching closely and carefully for you to get specific to the case. Stick with what you know about sexual abuse in general.)

If the client is someone with whom you have worked exclusively in a specific area such as sexual abuse, and you have experience and training in that area, then testimony may be appropriate. But before agreeing to testify, always ask the following questions:

1. Does this attorney know who I am and what I do?
2. Does he know how to qualify me as an expert in this area?
3. Have I ever been qualified as an expert in this area?
4. When and how many times?
5. Will the attorney know how to overcome objections to my expertise?
6. Has the attorney ever questioned an expert in this area?
7. Would it be more appropriate to be qualified as an expert in conducting biopsychosocial assessments and giving opinions about my conclusions?
8. Do I have enough information about my client to give the results of a biopsychosocial assessment, or do I have enough time to gather that information?
9. If I am qualified as an expert in sexual abuse, will it limit the amount of important information that I can provide for the court about this client?
10. Can this attorney ask for a continuance in order to allow time to do this properly?

If you know that your client's case may turn into a legal matter or it is a legal matter from the outset, do not hesitate to call the attorney frequently, ask questions, and get to know the attorney's secretary or paralegal. Be a constant reminder to them that being professional means not waiting until the last minute.

Stanley Brodsky gives a most helpful example of a telephone conversation with an indifferent attorney who is content with discussing your case in the courthouse hallway just prior to your testimony (Brodsky, 1991, p. 96):

> **ATT:** Don't be a worrywart. I have the case in hand. We don't have to meet.
> **WIT:** That's not okay.
> **ATT:** Listen, I have had dozens of cases just like this. I'll just see you in court.
> **WIT:** That's not okay.
> **ATT:** What's the matter with you? Are you panicking?
> **WIT:** It's important that we meet and go over my testimony. It's not okay just to meet in court.
> **ATT:** Let's do this; I will call you if we need to meet.
> **WIT:** I appreciate that offer, but that's not okay. I can schedule a meeting after working hours the evening before the hearing, and I can come by your office if that would be more convenient.
> **ATT:** I guess that will be okay.

Brodsky explains that even this approach does not always work, and anything from "simple insistence to mild threats" may be required to bring around a recalcitrant attorney. I have sent letters to attorneys outlining the deficiencies I see in the way he is handling my part of the case. I might list failure to meet, refusal to provide records, or treatment of the client as possible reasons to withdraw from the case if changes are not made. Are you hurting the client by withdrawing from the case? You are probably hurting the client by staying and allowing yourself to be manipulated by a bad attorney. As Brodsky notes, some attorneys are not indifferent but incompetent. Their degree of incompetency will help you determine whether to decline the case or try to educate them (Brodsky, 1991).

I do not tell lawyer jokes, and certainly every profession has its problems. Clinical social workers have not escaped categorizations but the public seems to have placed lawyers on a plane of their own. Certainly some of the criticisms are justified, and some are not. Because we are not trained in the law, there is much that we do not understand about legal issues in particular cases.

Most of the lawyers I have known have been dedicated advocates, and have both legal and interpersonal instincts that make them effective in the courtroom. Working with them was a pleasurable experience. Unfortunately, some bad experiences can be recalled in great detail. The best lessons come from those horrific experiences, and much of my courtroom demeanor has been shaped by those bad moments on the witness stand. Now, it only takes me about thirty seconds on the telephone to identify a potentially troublesome attorney.

Let me share some circumstances under which I have worked with attorneys. I once tried to explain my conclusions to a lawyer who was constantly running out the door to consult with construction workers building a gazebo outside his office where he was to wed in a few days. I have tried to go over my opinions with an attorney who was closing on his home, one who was planning a bar mitzvah, another who was trying to make it to the hospital in time for the birth of his child, and one who was test driving her new BMW.

They are funny, maddening, bright and not so bright, disoriented and disorienting. They perceive social workers as vague, wishy-washy, and noncommittal. If you are going to go to court, you have to learn to deal with lawyers effectively. Many attorneys dislike me because I do not cater to their demands. I never hesitate to let them know that I will not change my mind during testimony and give the answer they want. Many times the real problem is settling down attorneys long enough to hear what testimony can be given honestly and truthfully, thus helping them to understand the significance of my conclusions. Others continue to call because they know they will receive a thorough assessment of their client, which helps them to make better decisions on how to conduct their cases. Most experts never get the opportunity in court to explain the number of cases that they refuse. It is important for the court to understand that we are present in court because we have something significant to say about the client. There are many clients for whom our intervention is not appropriate.

Finally, a word about judges. Most of the judges I have appeared before have been very professional. Some get a little sleepy, some shuffle through papers, and others can be a tad grumpy at times. I once had a family court judge launch into a tirade in the middle of my testimony. He was angry about therapists who expressed opinions on where a child should be placed after interviewing only one parent in a child custody case. I could not agree with him more, but he had not waited to hear my conclusions (which addressed this issue) before jumping on his soapbox. I later wrote to him and suggested an advisory committee to address this issue as well as court-appointed experts who would assess the entire family. The judge replied that he had no time for that sort of thing, and that it would not be appropriate for a judge to be involved in such a committee. The truth was that he knew the lawyers would have a fit! They earn their living on the adversarial system. What would happen if we all mediated and came to a compromise? There goes the system as they prefer it.

Attorneys play a "devil's advocate" game when you first meet with them. To the uninitiated, the attorney appears to be the cross-examiner as he fires questions, tries to confuse you, intimidates, and generally acts like a complete jerk. At some point in law school, law students learn this method of testing their own witnesses. It is a terrible idea, and I have been through it more times than I care to remember.

The very worst experience I had with the "devil's advocate" test was with an extremely hyperactive attorney who blazed into the room with a huge video camera set on his shoulder and began firing sniper-style questions at the experts who were well-trained, experienced professionals. They had been on the stand before and knew what to expect both on direct examination and cross-examination. This attorney succeeded in doing nothing more that creating confusion, tension, anxiety, and blank stares. The attorney created a scenario so unlikely that even the most seasoned witness would have simply shut down. This is not the best way to test witnesses, whether they are lay witnesses or experts. My reaction to this exercise was to become very calm and to use quiet self-talk. It was important to know that what he was doing was not going to happen in the courtroom. He was actually having fun at our expense. He believed that experiencing this exercise would somehow make us better witnesses. It was an incredible waste of time and embarrassing for those of us who know how to handle ourselves professionally on the witness stand. Imagine the impact this had on the lay witnesses who were probably having this one and only experience in court.

Interestingly, during the trial, this same attorney changed course in midstream and cornered me in the witness room with the same rapid-fire style while explaining his latest great strategy. I responded as I had in his office—no response at all. I watched him, listened to him, and quietly and calmly focused on breathing, refusing to become agitated right before testifying. I would just do the best I could. As predicted, none of the questions he had feared were asked upon cross-examination. But his aggressive style infected everyone. A colleague who has had many years of experience in court recommends that difficult attorneys be treated as if they were clients. It helps you to muster up some empathy and compassion for them while remaining patient and calm.

Most attorneys are willing to work with you if you assert yourself professionally. They like to be able to visualize information, but never make the assumption that they are listening to you at all times. When you speak to an attorney, his mind is racing toward the legal ramifications of what you have to say and how your opinions will play out in the courtroom. If the opinions formed do not meet with his themes for the case, he always has the option not to use you. In fact, he has a duty to make good decisions about expert witnesses.

WORKING WITH THE LAWYER ON YOUR CASE: SUMMARY

1. If the attorney does not call you in time to prepare conclusions and opinions, tell him you need more time. If you have been working with a client for a while and you feel you can give an opinion, then prepare to testify. Be sure you can support your opinions. Insist on at least one meeting with the at-

torney before going to court. Make it clear to the attorney that you want his undivided attention.

2. Never let an attorney persuade you to give testimony you are not comfortable with. Not only is this a violation of ethics, but it can cause trouble for you on cross-examination as well.

3. Make sure the attorney understands who you are and what you do so he can defend your expertise. If you are using the biopsychosocial assessment, make sure he knows what the assessment is and why it is important.

Chapter 4

Investigators and Investigations

Some investigators are trained and experienced and some are not. Some specialize in certain types of cases and some take all cases. Many private investigators are former police officers who are either retired or investigating part-time. Frequently, clinical social workers are retained by attorneys or are court ordered to conduct investigations into various legal matters. The clinical social workers bring to investigations the interview and relationship-building skills that come from their highly specialized social work training. They know how to ask questions in ways that are more likely to elicit the information needed. They know the importance of taking their time and engendering trust. Clinical social workers bring to the legal arena knowledge of human behavior that is drawn from a more comprehensive view of the individual or family. Investigators from other backgrounds simply do not know what they are doing and can actually damage your chances of getting the information you need.

The history of social work strongly supports the role of social worker as investigator (Barker and Branson, 1993). As Barker and Branson have noted, social workers have been conducting investigations and reporting their findings in court since the turn of the century. Social work investigation is as old as the profession itself. Barker and Branson explain that it was natural for social work to have close ties to the law and legal justice system. In their book, *Forensic Social Work*, they write that it was not until the mid-1930s that social workers turned away from a legal orientation and moved in the directions of mental health and humanistic concerns.

Prior to that time, social workers and lawyers worked closely, especially in the areas of victimization and corrections.

Barker now sees social work as a new specialty focusing on the legal and humanistic service systems. He lists expert testimony, investigating cases of possible criminal conduct, child custody, divorce, delinquency, nonsupport, and mental hospital commitment among those activities appropriate to social work expertise. Although his writings are focused more on legal issues that impact the social work profession, his history of social work and the law are worth reviewing. I have found this history to be useful on the witness stand when questioned about the role of social work experts in the courtroom.

In an interesting case in a southern state, the judge decided that social workers were not experts. In fact, he asked what a social worker was and whether that particular state had any. He stopped the proceeding to consult his law books, and found that indeed, social workers were considered expert witnesses and could be qualified as such. The following demonstrates how knowledge of the history of social work investigations and testimony in court can establish credibility when the profession is being questioned:

Q. Ms. Vogelsang, is social work considered a profession?

A. Yes, it is, and one with a long history.

Q. Have social workers been testifying in court for very long?

A. Oh yes. Actually since the late nineteenth century. About one hundred years.

Q. What kind of things do they testify about?

A. The list is rather long. They testify about victimization, poverty and deprivation, family violence, child development, child abuse, battered women, and many other behavioral and environmental issues that affect people's lives.

Q. Do they testify about offenders or perpetrators, both juvenile and adults?

A. Yes. Social workers have an equally long history in corrections.

Q. What has the role of the social worker been in the courtroom?

A. Social workers have historically been either investigator, reporting findings to the court, and/or expert witness, interpreting those findings and offering expert opinions to the court.

Many investigators are fascinated by what they learn while working with a clinical social worker. However, some investigators are resistant to our requests; they do not understand why the information we seek is important. These encounters are opportunities to educate investigators on a number of issues that cause them to suddenly take greater interest in the case and the client. Some investigators truly have social work instincts, even though they have no social work training. It is a bonus to get one of these dedicated individuals to gather records and find people for you.

CHECKLIST FOR INVESTIGATIONS

It is a good idea to mail or fax the checklist for investigators (see Example 3) to the attorney and the investigator at the very beginning of most types of cases. I inform him or her that this is the most basic information needed, and that these records and my interviews may require additional records or interviews. I find that this list is most appreciated; it gives the attorney and the investigator some direction. Otherwise, they have only a vague idea of what you do and what you want. After all, they asked you to conduct the assessment because you are the expert.

Every item in Example 3 may not always apply to every case you have. But it is amazing when some obscure piece of information gleaned from an old record has given me insight into areas of an individual's life that I might never have questioned otherwise. Depending on the nature of my case, I may mark through some of

EXAMPLE 3. Checklist for Investigations

TO: NAME OF ATTORNEY OR INVESTIGATOR
RE: PRELIMINARY CHECKLIST FOR INVESTIGATION ON (CASE NAME)

1. Birth certificates for client, parents, children, spouse, siblings, grand-parents.
2. Birth records from hospital and physicians, including mother's prenatal care for client, siblings.
3. Early childhood medical records including family physician records. If no family physician, check public clinics in communities where family lived for all family medical records. Check every hospital in areas where family lived; look especially for emergency room records for client, client's mother (battering incidents), client's siblings.
4. Medical records for any hospitalization or hospital treatment. Always check emergency rooms in every geographic area where client lived. Ask specifically for films of any X rays, CT scans, MRIs as well as narrative reports.
5. School records. Check each school attended as well as school board. Ask school board or schools if outside private or public agencies conducted psychological evaluations or special testing. Contact those agencies and obtain their records also. Review school yearbooks and publications.
6. Parents' marriage certificates for all marriages.
7. Parents' divorce records for all divorces, child support orders, custody decrees, peace bonds/temporary restraining orders. Obtain attorney files for divorce.
8. Client's marriage certificates.
9. Client's divorce records.
10. Police response calls and incident reports to residences where family lived.
11. Social service agencies for AFDC payments, home studies, referral for testing and counseling, interventions, placement in foster homes, termination of parental rights.
12. Department of youth services for records, reports, evaluations, testing, counseling, intervention, placement, treatment for client and all siblings.
13. Juvenile facilities. Check each facility as well as central agency for all medical, intake, evaluation, disciplinary, schooling records.
14. Private social service agencies. Check with Catholic Social Services, private juvenile shelter, Big Brothers and Big Sisters, Boys' and Girls' Clubs, and other private agencies for any records on the client or siblings.
15. Obtain military records on client and other family members.
16. Death certificates and death records. Get autopsy and hospital records for any family member who died. Get obituary.
17. Prior jail records. Obtain local jail records for each arrest and incarceration for client, siblings, parents. Include medical records as well as conduct records.
18. Check with each prison as well as central office of Department of Corrections. Ask for medical as well as institutional records.

19. Current jail records. Check jail weekly for institutional and medical records, including medication charts, disciplinary reports, cell changes, visitors. If referred to outside health care facility, obtain those medical records.
20. Employment records. Check for salary, work accidents, attendance, performance evaluations.
21. Adult education. Check with Job Corps, Urban League, private agencies, community colleges, GED programs.
22. FBI. Obtain all FBI records, including rap sheets, previous investigations.
23. State law enforcement records. Obtain rap sheet, previous investigations.
24. Prior criminal records including arrest, charges, convictions. Obtain all records from prior counsel (including attorney work product), complete court file, prosecution file, incarceration records.
25. Psychiatric records for client and family members who received mental health treatment or were hospitalized. If hospitalization was involuntary, obtain court records.
26. Probation and parole. Get all probation and parole records. Check with local parole office as well as regional and central office.
27. Records of awards, recognitions, trophies, accomplishments.
28. News articles either positive or negative on client.
29. Any investigations or reports on institutions or programs in which the client was involved.
30. Housing records.

these items before sending the list to the attorney or investigator. I operate upon the maxim that one can never have too much information!

Do not forget that you must have signed releases for both the information you are seeking and to speak with certain people. You can adapt this list to the circumstances of your case.

Unfortunately, some investigators locate one record and believe you have enough. They will explain sincerely that records have been purged, lost in floods, fires, or tornadoes (sometimes they really have been lost this way). They might tell you that they sent a letter requesting the documents and are quite satisfied with the response that no records exist. Ask the investigator to go to the location where the records are housed, be nice with the record keepers, and try again even if it does not work the first time. It is amazing how much depends on who you work with in locating records and people. Persistence is the key to a good investigator.

If the investigator is not getting the job done, call the attorney and send a written "to do list" stating that you must have those documents or access to those people before you can testify. Documents and people often magically appear!

One of the more annoying habits of investigators, whether social workers or other credentialed investigators, is their refusal to read maps, lay out directions, and locate interviewees (and record directions to their locations) before taking you to the interview or to the community. I also greatly resent side trips to find documents, which just happen to be on the way to the next interview. On the other hand, those side trips have given me the opportunity to demonstrate to investigators the correct questions to be asked in order to obtain certain records. For example, most non-social work investigators know very little about social services records. They are satisfied to get one or two face sheets when hundreds of pages are probably stored somewhere at that office or on computers. They are equally as puzzled as to why eligibility records would be significant in a child abuse case. As an expert witness in court cases, numerous opportunities exist to educate everyone involved.

Investigators must make a living and they are usually working on many cases at the same time, not just yours. Organizing and prioritizing your list of needed documents is one way to ensure prompt attention to your case. Asking family members to obtain as many records as possible also lightens the load of the investigator. Family members are especially good with procuring school, medical, and employee records. More information on records will be discussed in Chapter 6.

There have been moments when an investigator's advice should have been heeded and when my natural fearlessness turned to foolishness. Badly in need of videotape of the area of a neighborhood where my client had lived, I persuaded an investigator to take me there in the middle of the day, thinking we would be safe. He forewarned me that he absolutely would not get out of the car, and it would not be safe for me to do so either. It seemed impossible to me that my usually successful, friendly demeanor would not work, but what the fellows on the corner wanted was my video camera. Fortunately, they only chased us on their bikes, but they were pretty fast. Our car could not travel quickly down narrow streets with heavy foot traffic. The investigator was gracious enough to not hit me over the head because of my poor judgment.

Investigators are perfectly capable of videotaping or photographing people and places. The clinical social worker does not need to be there. I go because I am positive that my social work training and background will be responsible for my seeing something significant, which the investigator may not think is important. Photographs of filthy bathrooms, broken windows, glass-strewn yards, overflowing trash cans, and roach-infested hallways speak so much more loudly and clearly than my words to a judge or a jury.

Some clinical social workers both investigate cases and serve as social work experts on the same cases. They track down witnesses, conduct interviews, find records, deal with legal issues, and then testify about their findings. My opinion is that as clinical social workers we should not wear both hats. The types of cases in which clinical social workers act in both capacities raise ethical issues of bias on the witness stand, especially if you are receiving fees for both activities. Other ethical issues will probably arise and it will be the responsibility of those of us who practice forensic social work to lead the way in exploring these issues. In the meantime, my advice is to wear one hat. It is exciting that there is a place for us either as experts or investigators. These fields are growing as the courts recognize our special skills. We may be increasingly called upon as admissions to schools of social work are growing, while admissions to the field of psychology and psychiatry are either static or dwindling. Because of our training and our approach to human behavior, we are appropriate for the courts. The courts need both our investigations and our testimony, but usually not both from the same social worker.

ASKING FOR AN INVESTIGATOR

If you are worried about the time required to do a thorough biopsychosocial assessment, remember that you do not need to track down people and records. Most attorneys who take family and criminal court cases have two or three investigators they can call upon if needed. Some larger firms hire their own investigators who have offices right in the lawyers' suite. Both prosecutors and public defenders have investigators, though unfortunately they are usually overworked and underpaid. I always ask the attorney if he has an investigator because if he wants a thorough biopsychosocial assessment of the client, he must allow me to meet with the investigator and submit a list of people and records I will need.

INVESTIGATORS AND INVESTIGATIONS: SUMMARY

1. It is probably best to wear only one hat. Either investigate your case or agree to be the social work expert directing and using the information gathered. Try not to do both.
2. Ask the attorney on your case if she has an investigator who can gather records and find people important to your case. If she says no, tell her it will be impossible for you to conduct a thorough assessment without one.
3. Send the checklist for investigation to the lawyer and the investigator. If the lawyer does not have an investigator, she will probably pass the list to her paralegal or secretary.
4. Meet with the client and his or her family. Provide a list of records and people important to your case. Divide the tasks of locating both.
5. Ask the investigator to go back more than once to places that refuse records. Have the records court ordered if necessary.

Chapter 5

Interviews

From the moment you first see a client whose case is going to court, it is most helpful to use the biopsychosocial assessment as your framework for gathering information. This will make your preparation for court a much less anxious experience, and provides a way of pacing your time. You can adapt this framework to your particular case even if you plan to be qualified as an expert in an area other than conducting biopsychosocial assessments.

After you have had your initial meeting with the client who is going to court, you want to begin a list of others associated with the client who might warrant interviews. Why? It does in fact increase your credibility in the courtroom if you did not rely solely on the information obtained from the client or even the family members. Yes, you are perfectly capable of drawing upon your skills to form opinions concerning what you have learned about this person. Perhaps you are even a social worker with some testing skills and you are using those as well. But you are still subject upon cross-examination to the suggestion that you are just another paid expert who believes everything you are told.

A few interviews with nonfamily members, along with records that support the information obtained in the interviews, will give you more credibility as an expert witness. It is important to interview family members who know your client well because no one grows up in a vacuum. It is important to learn about those who were close to your client, to observe their behavior as well, and obtain their perspectives on your client. Other possible interviews might include doctors, neighbors, employers, co-workers, friends, and teachers. Teachers and school counselors often lend keen observations regarding the client.

The clinical social worker has a skill that is rarely found in other professionals—a profound understanding of how terribly anxious the client feels and how long it takes to establish a trusting relationship with a client. Building that trust should be first and foremost in establishing the interviewing environment (Lukas, 1993). Under the best of circumstances it is not easy for a client to seek help, therapy, or counseling. In a legal situation, the anxiety is intensified because the client must discuss personal matters that he or she would never have had to reveal otherwise. The client does not know you, does not necessarily trust you, and sometimes does not understand why he or she needs to reveal certain information.

This is why attorneys, psychiatrists, and psychologists often miss vital pieces of information that might be important to a case. Other professionals can rarely sit for four or five hours at one time in their own offices, much less in a home or apartment where the TV and stereo are blaring, there is no air conditioning, various un-identified creatures are milling about, and children and neighbors are screaming. And let us not exclude prisons, hospitals, juvenile detention centers, and other facilities that can be noisy, crowded, and poorly ventilated. If you are a private practitioner and have become accustomed to seeing people only in your office for one-hour sessions, then certain court cases will quickly reunite you with your broader social work training and mission of assessing clients on their own turf. This will enable you to bring a much-needed perspective into the courtroom.

We are trained to allow people the time they need to be frustrated, angry, oppositional, resistant, and just plain obnoxious until they see that we are actually listening, speaking in a quiet voice, respecting their perceptions even if we personally don't agree, asking caring questions, and taking whatever time needed to gain their trust. Attorneys tend to be very direct; then they wonder why the client does not immediately open up to them. Psychiatrists tend to use language the client does not understand. Psychologists frequently establish just enough of a relationship to complete testing. Many times they do not bother to form any trust with the client at all, and the client goes into the testing anxious and intimidated, which can affect testing outcomes.

Clinical social workers learn interview skills that get clients to talk to them in a very different way from others, and much of that concerns patience. We know that it took a great deal of time and multiple experiences to get the client to the present situation. We are not going to learn everything we need to know in one or two interviews.

The clinical social worker needs to be able to explain to the court why interviewing the client is important and, even more crucial, why it is important to interview others who knew the client at various times in his life. Again, we do not grow up in a vacuum. We are shaped by those who reared us, by neighbors, teachers, ministers, scout leaders, and many others. We must interview these people and be prepared in court to explain why it was important to do so.

One of the most difficult things to determine in an assessment is whether or not the client is malingering or outright lying. There is no foolproof method of making this determination, and this is where the clinical social work expert has an advantage in her testimony. Because we are not relying soley on the interview with the client, we can provide other sources to the court that show why we either believe or disbelieve the client (Rogers, 1997).

Most clients will report that they did pretty well in school. "Pretty well" lies somewhere between awful and great. It is embarrassing and humiliating to admit that you were not a good student. In most cases, there are very good reasons as to why clients did not do well, but they have never had that reason explained to them. They have usually walked around for years just thinking they were not very bright. Obtaining school records and talking to teachers can often clarify the truth about the client's school performance, which provides a piece of the puzzle regarding his current situation. Many of our clients are accused of lying when they are actually learning disabled (Copeland and Love, 1995), embarrassed, of low intellectual capacity, or ashamed. We must read the records in order to detect the accuracy of the client's statements. The clinical social worker should never assume that the information given in an interview is 100 percent correct. But the information is important as it is presented because it is filtered through the experiences in that person's life and it tells how the interviewee perceives the world. The interviews also provide the information needed to track down records that will substantiate the life experiences of the client.

SAMPLE INTERVIEW WITH A MOTHER

SW: Mrs. Jones, you and your family live so close to the canals. (observation made while driving through the neighborhood)

CLIENT: Oh, yes. Eleven kids have drowned in that canal over the years.

SW: Did Johnny know any of those kids?

CLIENT: No. But you know . . . and I hadn't thought of this in years . . . but his Aunt Mae, my youngest sister, got drunk one night and had Johnny and his sister in the car, and they went right into that canal. They all got out, went to the ER, and were checked out by the doctors. They were OK. Except you know, Johnny 'til this day comes home a different way where he doesn't have to go by that canal. We tease him about it. And he did have nightmares for a long time after that.

SW: Mrs. Jones, his friend Ronnie says that they knew some of the kids that drowned in the canal. Ronnie says they saw one kid pulled out and worked on by paramedics and then covered with a sheet.

CLIENT: You know now, you are asking me to go back a long way and I was at work all the time. Maybe he did know some of those kids. They all ran around the neighborhood together. The city came out and said they were going to put some rails up, but they never did. Actually, we did go to the funeral of that one child . . . what was his name? You ask Johnny, because I believe we did know that child.

This brief snippet of conversation resulted in a slew of emergency room records, accident reports, news articles, and city documents. It also confirmed that the client had both experienced and witnessed some terrifying events as a child. Testimony from this interview was significant in establishing that the client had suffered traumatic situations and loss in childhood.

SAMPLE INTERVIEW WITH MILITARY PERSONNEL

SGT: Truthfully ma'am, he cried most of the time we were in the Middle East. He wanted to go so he could live up to the image of his father who died in Vietnam. He was so scared.

SW: Why do you think he was scared?

SGT: I don't know. He never saw any action, but he sure acted like someone who had. I never could figure that out. I know he grew up in a real poor neighborhood in a tough part of New York.

SW: Did he ever talk to you about that?

SGT: Not really. I do remember him saying once that he saw more bullets flying on the way to school than he had seen during this conflict. Said he never slept at night cause he was so scared. Maybe having to be on guard all the time reminded him of those days.

This interview led to military records, news articles about the housing projects where the client grew up, testimony by witnesses from the projects, videotapes of the projects, and additional interviews with community activists from that neighborhood.

Interviews provide a road map for other people, places, and things. The other people, places, and things lead to more interviews that lead to more people, places, and things. Some people will refuse to talk to you no matter how skilled you are at gaining trust. It is usually best to try twice and then let it go. Sometimes, that most difficult person will call you later and turn out to be your best interview. That person might also be paranoid, untreated, and dangerous. It is wise to stay aware and to use good judgement.

INTERVIEWS: SUMMARY

1. Interview as many of the following as you possibly can:
   - Parents and stepparents
   - Siblings
   - Grandparents and great grandparents
   - Aunts, uncles, and cousins
   - Neighbors, friends, girlfriends, and boyfriends
   - Teachers, coaches, principals, and school counselors
   - Employers and co-workers
   - Police officers, corrections officials (discuss with attorney first)
   - Ministers, Sunday school teachers, and social workers
   - Military officers and buddies
   - Other gang members
2. Have these people come to your office, interview by phone, or, best of all, go to where they reside.
3. When possible, work closely with an investigator to find others who knew your client and will share some information.
4. Be patient in the interviews; be prepared for resistance, anger, and anxiety. Listen quietly because many people will anticipate that you are not listening and are calmed when they realize you are not rushing them.
5. Go for the details no matter how long it takes or how often you must return for more interviews.
6. Adapt your language to the individual being interviewed.
7. Use your clinical skills to question and assess.
8. Use a checklist to make sure you have covered every possible base.

Chapter 6

Records

It has become increasingly important to gather as many documents as possible in order to substantiate findings from interviews. No longer are juries and judges content to take the word of an "expert" just because he has been qualified as such. They want to see how you reached your conclusions, what steps you took, how thorough your assessment was, and how you support your findings. "How do you know what you know?" (Brodsky, 1991) is the crucial question experts should ask themselves before going to court. Brodsky writes that "a lucid link should exist between the conclusions and the means of reaching those conclusions. Experience or education are never sufficient answers by themselves" (p. 98). You can certainly rely on your training and experience, but you are likely to have a much tougher time on cross-examination if that is the only support you can lend to your opinions. Social workers have a particularly heavy burden in this area because we are often perceived as "do-gooders" with a ready-made bias toward the client.

Because each side has its experts, it is easy to understand why jurors get confused. Sometimes they are given a lot of information to absorb; it must seem as if the testimony is just one expert's word against another. The advantage that the clinical social worker has with the biopsychosocial assessment is that he is able to say, "While I certainly rely on the information I learned from the client, as well as my experience and training in interviewing clients, I believe as you do that accuracy and consistency of this information is important. That is why I read records that relate to my client, consult with other experts involved with the client, interview others who knew him, and look for research or literature that supports or questions my findings. I, too, want the most thorough and consistent information possible before forming any opinions about the client."

What records are you looking for and how do you get them? If you are automatically worrying about the time it is going to take, quickly review the steps usually taken:

1. The client comes to your office and signs releases.
2. He takes releases to others you have listed for him (family members, employers, schools, etc.).
3. Some releases are mailed to various agencies (military, hospitals, etc.).
4. Either the client or your office secretary, or both, work on first getting releases signed and then off to the appropriate places.
5. Call the attorney on this case and discuss releases and records with her:
    a. Does she have an investigator?
    b. Can her paralegal handle the releases and records-gathering? (This is especially important if your client is in jail, prison, the hospital, etc.)

Maintain a "to do list" from the moment you accept a case that is going to court, or as soon as one of your regular clients finds himself in a legal situation that may require your involvement. List people and records that might be significant in your testimony, and check them off as you interview them or receive those records. The "I don't have time" excuse is simply unacceptable when you have a client in a legal situation. As professional social workers, we have a professional, ethical, and moral obligation to do our assessments no matter how much time is required. Otherwise, we do not earn the right to take the stand and call ourselves experts.

Records are treasure chests of information. Why shouldn't you trust that the client will remember everything that is significant in her life as she perceives it and is willing to share that with you? You have worked hard to establish trust, and you believe that you have established a strong therapeutic relationship with the client. The following are but a few of the legitimate reasons clients cannot tell you everything you need to know, especially in preparation for court:

- Learning disabilities that include difficulties with expressive and receptive language, auditory processing, and other types of information processing problems that affect communication.
- Memory loss.
- Attention deficit disorder with or without hyperactivity.
- Head injuries (which may exist without ever having been identified).
- Seizure activity that may not be easily recognizable and can often be misidentified as dissociation.
- Dissociation.
- Mental retardation. Those in the mild range often appear quite normal on the surface with extreme difficulty in processing information. Most have learned to compensate and appear more competent that they really are (Luckkason and Ellis 1985).
- Paranoia (often missed as a block to communication). We social workers often give the benefit of the doubt to paranoid clients in our eagerness to allow for the natural suspiciousness many clients have about our questioning their personal lives.

Many organic and nonorganic reasons cause clients to withhold significant information. Records give us the opportunity to clarify information and to explore new information. Records validate or negate information from interviews. They also can lead to new and important information. It is reassuring as an expert witness to know that you can rely on your experience and training as well as documentation that supports your findings. You are building on the credibility of what you have learned, and your expertise in conducting biopsychosocial assessments is guiding your findings and conclusions.

SAMPLE OF DIRECT TESTIMONY FROM RECORDS

Q. Ms. Vogelsang, you stated earlier that gathering records and other documents are part of the biopsychosocial assessment. Could you briefly review the significance of the records as they relate to a client?

A. Yes. While I certainly rely on information from interviews, I look for additional information on clients from records in order to gather new information, clarify old information, and to seek consistency of information.

Q. And did you review records that revealed information about Mr. Jones?

A. Yes, I did.

Q. Could you just briefly list the records you reviewed for this case?

A. Yes. I reviewed Mr. Jones's birth records (name hospital and dates), pediatric records (name doctors and dates), school records (name schools and dates), and his military records (branch of service and dates).

Q. Could you tell the court please what you learned from Mr. Jones's pediatric records?

A. Yes. There was early and ongoing treatment for numerous ear infections and sore throats. By the age of six, Dr. Smith was already noting an increase in motor activity suggestive of hyperactivity. By age eight, Dr. Smith began noting his discussions with the parents regarding medication for Mr. Jones's behavior. Subsequent notes record his responsiveness to the medication and other behavioral indications of improvement.

Q. What is the significance of the information in this record to you?

A. First, it confirms the information I was given in interviews with Mr. Jones's parents. But more important, the records describe the early signs and symptoms of behaviors that would most likely reoccur when his parents discontinued treatment at age nine, against medical advice.

Q. What happened when the medication was discontinued?

A. Mr. Jones's school performance dropped and his behavior became unmanageable in the classroom.

Q. How do you know that?

A. In addition to interviewing the teacher who had Mr. Jones in her class, I read his school records. It is clear that his drop in school performance and his change in behavior corresponds with notes made by the teacher at that time, along with her recommendations for counseling.

Q. Ms. Vogelsang, do you have an opinion as to the impact of stopping the successful treatment of Mr. Jones?

A. Yes. Because the treatment was stopped, Mr. Jones began to fail in most subjects. The teacher was constantly sending him to the principal's office, and his unpleasant behavior toward the other children made them fearful of him. They both ridiculed and avoided him at the same time. As a result, Mr. Jones became even more aggressive and assaultive toward others. His parents refused to take the advice of the school and the doctors, and by the end of the school year, Mr. Jones had failed in all classes and had to be retained. It is important to note that psychologically, this situation creates a great deal of shame and humiliation in a child. Self-worth and self-esteem are destroyed and the child's image of himself becomes the same as the one seen by others. Without immediate and meaningful intervention, this pattern continues and can become a way of life.

Q. (The next question would pull in research, literature, studies, and a theoretical basis for these conclusions. Then interviews with any other experts or professionals who had assessed Mr. Jones or who had expertise in this type of behavior would be discussed. Finally, teacher notes and/or a chart showing the school or medical records might be presented depending on the type of case being heard.)

SAMPLE OF CROSS-EXAMINATION
ON THE RECORDS

Q. Ms. Vogelsang, this parent is going to say anything to show herself in a good light because she wants custody of this child. How do you know how much she earns and where she lives and what activities she attends with this child other that what she has told you?

A. In addition to interviewing her employer and the property manager at her apartment complex, I asked for copies of her employee evaluations, confirmed her salary, asked that she provide me with statements from her son's Scout leader and Little League coach. I also ran a check with the Department of Social Services and found that she had never been reported for child abuse, and I ran a check with South Carolina Law Enforcement Division (SLED) and found no arrests or prior convictions. I have copies of those documents with me if you would like the court to review them.

SAMPLE OF DIRECT TESTIMONY IN A SEXUAL ABUSE CASE

Q. Ms. Vogelsang, how do you personally know that Mr. Smith sexually abused this child? Were you there to see it? Aren't you just taking the word of her mother?

A. While it is true that I was not personally present to observe Mr. Smith sexually abusing this child, I am convinced from the information in her medical records, along with her father's prior arrests for molestation of other children, that we must take this claim very seriously. She has certainly been molested and, in my opinion, she is not safe with him in the home.

I have been amazed at the number of times a case has been agreed upon in lawyers' offices and in court hallways because the other side realized how powerful those records would be if presented properly before the judge. It is also appalling that lazy or uninterested attorneys frequently fail to ask for documentation.

I generally take the documents that I will rely on to court with me. Depending on the nature of the case, this may be a manila folder with files, a portfolio of files, or a box of files with hanging folders clearly marked for easy access. The use of these documents on the stand will be discussed more fully in Chapter 12 on direct testimony. But it does bear repeating that you do not want to fumble around on the stand. Records need to be well organized, easily pulled from their files, and sections easily referenced.

Just as your client-attorney wants to know your opinion and what you base it on, the opposing attorney also wants to know (Poynter, 1987). Poynter recommends that you treat everything you write or have in your files as discoverable. Discovery is "A modern pre-trial procedure by which one party gains information held by another party" (Gifis, 1991, p. 138). In the course of conducting your biopsychosocial assessment, remember that any notes you make, any records you use, and your visual aids are discoverable. While there may technically be exceptions to this rule, my advice is to be cautious and prudent in your assessments. Be ready to defend whatever you have recorded, read, or relied upon.

It is completely unacceptable to me to destroy records or dispose of them inappropriately after testifying in any legal matter. Although there are no general rules about maintaining records, our profession does address this issue (*NASW Code of Ethics,* 1996).

In one case, an appeal hearing was scheduled and I went about talking to individuals involved in the original trial, which took place about three years earlier. The social worker who had testified in the original trial had destroyed all of her records and could not understand why this was a problem for her former client. Keep all documentation, records, and visual aids from your court cases.

RECORDS: SUMMARY

1. Gather or gain access to as many records as possible. One seemingly unimportant record can have information that leads to other important records.
2. Read the records carefully. They often contain names, places, and events that lead to further information.

3. Do not take no for an answer. Most records are public information or must be turned over when a release is presented. Courts and hospitals are getting around providing records by charging outlandish fees. Impress upon the attorney how important it is to have these records. Sometimes she will need to get a court order.

4. Often the worst providers of records are Departments of Social Services. Insist that the attorney get a court order if necessary to obtain those records.

5. List the records you have reviewed. Highlight pertinent information. Remember that source of information in your testimony. Be prepared to explain why it lends credibility to information gathered in interviews.

6. Retain a copy of your records and notes.

Chapter 7

Interviewing Other Experts

Even though many experts are aware of the importance of the biopsychosocial assessment and want to know the family background before assessing the clients for themselves, others see no reason for the assessment. However, the DSM-IV assigns an axis for the biopsychosocial stressors (APA, 1994), and the impact of those stressors is supposed to be considered across all four axes. Some professionals prefer to go it alone, and in the process they hurt the client not only in treatment but in court as well. They certainly cannot give a judge or jury a complete view of the client without knowledge of the biopsychosocial assessment.

Always contact other experts or professionals who have evaluated the client in the past as well as those who are involved on the current legal case. The majority of experts are very cooperative and want to do a good job in court. Most experts share a genuine interest in the case. Those of us who choose to testify usually believe we have something to offer that would help the court in decision making.

Expert testimony has a ripple effect that impacts people in ways we never suspect. After nineteen years of testifying and leaving the courtroom after my time on the stand, I have been moved by the number of people who have walked up to me and said that my testimony had really made them think about their own behavior and how they were going to change the way they treat their child, spouse, or parent (or that they were going to seek help). I have been told this by jurors, judges, lawyers, bailiffs, court recorders, spectators, and reporters. Although we may not have an impact on the outcome of a case, we certainly do have an impact somewhere. This has kept me coming back to court where I know for sure that someone is going to leave changed in some significant way.

It is very important to get the attorney to provide you with a list of other experts from the very start. It is even better if the attorney calls you first for the biopsychosocial assessment and then, based on that assessment, makes a determination of what other experts are needed. I have often seen attorneys work from back to front and later realize that they have wasted a great deal of taxpayer or client money on experts they did not need. There are, of course, exceptions to this. For example, a known case of head injury with brain damage is going to call for medical doctors and neurological analysis. But I have seen far too many attorneys call in psychiatrists and psychologists when they needed an expert in mental retardation, substance abuse, psychopharmacology, or some other specialty.

When you call the other experts, tell them that you are conducting a biopsychosocial assessment on the client and you would like to share the information with them. If they reply that you should send them a report, tell them that you may not be preparing a report from your assessment and that it would be best if you could talk with them personally. If you have prepared a report, discuss with the client and the attorney whether you should send the report to anyone else. Sometimes the problem with sending a report to another expert is that it will get lost somewhere on his desk and never be read. Ask the other expert for a time when you can meet if you are in the same town. Ask the attorney to arrange a meeting at her office. It is even better if the attorney is there to absorb some of this information and to stay current on the findings.

Some uncooperative experts who waited until the day of my testimony to learn about my findings, have approached me afterward to say that they wished they had known my conclusions earlier because the information affected the way they now viewed the client. They then rush off to the hotel or to the attorney to rethink some of their own findings. I have had other experts say that my findings in the biopsychosocial assessment changed their diagnosis of the client or that it helped them to communicate better with the client, and enabled them to get to pertinent information faster and more effectively. They have also told me that hearing my assessment in the form of testimony gave them a broader view and one they would have never had otherwise.

If my findings are inconsistent with those of the other experts, I need to note that right away. An important clue may be discovered because of this inconsistency. For example, if the intelligence tests show an IQ of 118 and the school records show straight "F's," then I need to be able to explain why that happened. The answer usually can be found in teacher notes, teacher interviews, and school testing.

EXAMPLE OF TESTIMONY REGARDING OTHER EXPERTS

Q. Ms. Vogelsang, you said that your biopsychosocial assessment included interviewing other experts involved with Mr. Jones. Why is that important?

A. Again, with the biopsychosocial assessment, I am looking for consistency of information, or the lack thereof, in forming my opinions. If I learn in interviews that Mr. Jones was failing in school and another expert who had tested him found that he had an IQ of 120, then it would be of great importance to me to clarify the cause of that discrepancy.

Q. Did you also review the reports and findings of experts who have evaluated Mr. Jones?

A. Yes.

Q. And you heard one expert testify that Mr. Jones had passive-dependent traits that contributed to his behavior. Is that not correct?

A. Yes, I did.

Q. Are you testifying that the expert is wrong?

A. No. But Dr. Smith did not have the benefit of a complete biopsychosocial assessment and in my opinion was unaware of numerous significant factors in Mr. Jones's life that would explain the underlying appearance of passive-dependent traits.

Looking for consistency of information across a broad spectrum of data shows the court that you are not just accepting the information obtained in interviews, even though you have the clinical skills to assess that information and form opinions from what you have learned. Interviews with other experts and reviews of their reports add credibility to your findings, while whatever inconsistencies you find lead to further exploration.

In reviewing the records that come in on a client, it is important to note other professionals who may have assessed the client many years prior to the current legal situation. Do not hesitate to call social workers, medical doctors, probation officers, juvenile detention staff psychologists, and any others you find in records who have evaluated, tested, or simply made notes on daily observations of the client. This information can be most helpful in providing answers to your client's past functioning and how it compares to the present circumstances.

INTERVIEWING OTHER EXPERTS: SUMMARY

1. Interview other experts who have known or evaluated the client or who are currently involved in the legal case.
2. Provide as much family history and other information as the expert is willing to absorb. If they are not interested, let the attorney know that you see this as a problem.
3. Ask questions about the expert's evaluation. Compare your own findings.
4. Look for inconsistencies in your findings and that of other experts. Ascertain why those have occurred.
5. Ask for copies of all testing. This includes psychological evaluations, psychiatric evaluations, and the assessments of all other experts on the case as well as documentation from any professionals who have treated the client in the past.

Chapter 8

Research and Other Publications

You have probably noticed by now that through the biopsychosocial assessment the clinical social worker is building a sturdy foundation for her testimony by looking for consistency in the interviews, the records, and the findings of other experts. The fourth building block in this process is a search for literature and studies that relate to the client and the client's situation. Stanley Brodsky observes in his book on court testimony that, once on their own, many professionals read little, or they depend much more on their experience for knowledge. "They stay current in their field in a haphazard manner, reading articles here, attending workshops or seminars there, without an overall plan or conceptualization of what they need to know" (Brodsky, 1991, p. 11). It is crucial to be current in the area in which you have claimed expertise or on the subject about which you are testifying. My file cabinet is overflowing with publications and articles collected over the years including research and studies that I have used in court. As new information becomes available in a certain area, it is added to a collection that has served me well in court.

The Internet has become a home library for me. I have located numerous Web pages, Web sites, and other locations for finding the latest research, studies, publications, and journal articles on various subjects. These articles have led me to some very interesting people who have shared fascinating personal experiences through e-mail. I was researching the impact of exposure to certain metals in one case and ended up communicating with an individual who was an expert on the subject. He had been exposed to metal poisoning over a number of years and was also an advocate for greater worker protections for those who still work around metals. He was even more credible because he was president of a company that worked in metals. He was a tremendous guide in helping me find the latest research and literature on the subject. I used much of what I learned from him in my court testimony and had the very best references for that testimony.

If the client was in juvenile detention, then look for studies that describe the common denominators found in kids in detention. For example, I located a United States Department of Justice study that demonstrated the impact on children who witness family violence and the increased likelihood that they would become juvenile and adult criminal offenders. My client was one who had witnessed family violence throughout childhood, had been through the juvenile justice system, and was now an incarcerated adult. I had other studies similar to this one in order to ensure that this one study was not unusual or inconsistent with other research. Knowing that adolescents in juvenile detention have a high rate of learning disabilities, I reviewed studies that supported or negated that relationship in order to strengthen the consistency of my testimony.

Always try to contact authors of publications that relate to the client you are assessing, and talk with them about your case. This is an incredible learning and educational opportunity that will impact the way in which you view your other clients as well. I have even attended seminars that other experts are giving in order to gather more extensive information and research to present to the court. At the time of this writing, I am preparing for a case that involves extensive psychological evaluations that show chronic childhood impulsivity and severe anxiety. I spent two days at a seminar with a nationally known psychologist and researcher, and I was able to gather useful information and take copious notes. Even though I treat clients who are suffering from anxiety, I am not an expert on anxiety to the extent that I have done research in these areas. But I am an expert at conducting biopsychosocial assessments, and I have clinical experience in treating private clients with symptoms of anxiety. The assessment can allow me to present my findings to the court, and in that capacity I can tell the judge and jury what I learned that supports my conclusions.

Some publications are atypical in terms of document searches and literature review. For example, civil suits are filed against various institutions to which the client was admitted or newspaper articles written on various deaths, accidents, crimes, and monetary awards that may be pertinent to a client or family member. Again, these publications can lead to other bits of information and help us to build a picture of the client's life.

CASE EXAMPLE 1

In one case, I learned through interviews and records that the client had spent a number of years in "training schools." These were basically reform schools for juvenile delinquents who could not remain in mainstream schools. A very skilled investigator on the case discovered that a civil suit had been filed against these schools. The suits cited numerous abuses to the children incarcerated there. The courts found the allegations to be true, and the suit was settled when the state agreed to reform the entire system. It happened that the client had been incarcerated in one of those schools and had suffered horrible abuse at the hands of his keepers and other older children. His descriptions of those abuses during our interviews would have been practically useless in court without the existence of a civil suit, which confirmed that those abuses did occur to incarcerated children during that period of time. I will refer to this case again in Chapter 9 on visual aids.

SAMPLE OF TESTIMONY REGARDING PUBLICATION OF CIVIL SUIT

Q. Ms. Vogelsang, you stated that during your interviews you learned that the client was in the _____ training school. What is a training school?

A. Basically a reform school, even though the mandate of these schools originally was to provide more in the area of academics, job training, and counseling so that the juvenile was released with skills needed to do well in society.

Q. And did you review the civil suit filed against the state on behalf of the children detained in this facility?

A. Yes, I did.

Q. And why was this document significant to you in terms of your assessment?

A. First, the defendant in this case was incarcerated there during the period of years in which the investigation was conducted and so might have witnessed, or been victim of, the abuses that occurred there as he had stated in the interviews I held with him. Second, the legal document confirms that those abuses did occur to most of the children there, even though only six names were listed as plaintiffs. The findings indicate that the abuses were the potential consequences of any child housed there, and that any child there would have at the very least witnessed the violations that occurred.

Q. Did this document lead you to take any other actions in your assessment?

A. Yes. I had an investigator locate staff at the training school who remembered Mr. Jones.

Q. And what did you learn?

A. That two of the staff did in fact witness the abuse of Mr. Jones.

Q. And will some of those staff testify in this case or provide affidavits that you have reviewed?

A. Yes.

CASE EXAMPLE 2

In another legal case that involved the sexual abuse of an eight-year-old female, the work of Dr. Bessel van der Kolk and Dr. Judith Herman was used. Both have expertise in trauma and have written extensively on the subject. Both have done a thorough job of describing trauma symptoms (van der Kolk, 1988; Herman, 1992).

Although I could not testify as to whether this child had been molested repeatedly by an uncle who had no prior record of abuse, especially because there was no medical evidence, I could talk about behaviors reported by the family, and my own observations of this child in treatment. To strengthen my conclusion that the child had in fact been sexually abused, I compared the behavioral symptoms observed by myself, the family and other evaluators to the detailed symptoms listed in the literature by well-known experts in the fields of sexual abuse and trauma.

SAMPLE OF TESTIMONY USING LITERATURE ON SEXUAL TRAUMA

Q. Ms. Vogelsang, you stated that in conducting a biopsychosocial assessment, you review research, studies, publications, and such to determine what other experts have written on a particular subject. Did you do that in this case?

A. Yes.

Q. And what information did you locate and review in preparation for your testimony?

A. I reviewed the work of Dr. Bessel van der Kolk, a medical doctor who has written extensively on the subject of trauma in children and adults, and likewise the work of Dr. Judith Herman, a psychiatrist who has also published in this area.

Q. Now, could you begin by describing the symptoms you either learned about in your interviews, gleaned from the records, or observed in working with the Clark child?

A. (I would then review my clinical findings from that research by listing the symptoms and behaviors I had found.)

Q. Ms. Vogelsang, could you describe the symptoms and behaviors you have reviewed from the works of Dr. van der Kolk and Dr. Herman.

A. (I would then review those symptoms and behaviors as they apply to children. It would be effective at this point to have a chart or visual aid prepared for the court that demonstrates the testimony.)

Q. Ms. Vogelsang, based on your interviews, review of the records, and review of pertinent research and literature in

the area of sexual abuse and trauma, is it your opinion that
Susan Clark has in fact been sexually abused?

A. Yes.

Q. And at this time do you have an opinion as to who the
abuser might be?

A. At this point, that would only be speculation on my part.

It is important to be able to give the title, author, and even the page
number of the literature you have reviewed. I usually take my sources
to the courtroom with me because the judge will often ask for copies
of articles or names of books to review in making his decision. I also
include information from the literature on visual charts. The information must relate clearly to the issue at hand.

Research and literature should be carefully reviewed while bear-
ing in mind both the strengths and weaknesses of various studies.
Again, as a social worker, I look for consistency of information. The
body of literature that best fits the picture you are seeing with your
client can help to form the theoretical basis for your opinions and
conclusions.

RESEARCH AND OTHER PUBLICATIONS: SUMMARY

1. Look for research that both supports and negates your findings. Be prepared to explain studies that do not support your
   findings.
2. Be prepared to discuss the author of the research and the details of the findings. Do not worry about quoting page numbers, but politely state that you can get those if the court really
   wants them.
3. Attend seminars and workshops, and call upon information
   from those you have attended in the past if the information applies to your case. Contact the workshop speakers and ask for
   copies of their publications, bibliographies, and articles. Tell
   them about your case and ask questions.

4. Keep a file system on articles, publications, books, and research that apply to the types of cases you assess and stay current on those.
5. Look for legal briefs, lawsuits, and new articles that can substantiate your information from interviews.
6. If you cannot find research or literary support for your opinions, you should still rely on your clinical experience, training, and skills.

Chapter 9

Visual Aids

Visual aids are being used more frequently in the courtroom. This makes sense because we know that people are more likely to remember what they see than what they hear. Studies show that jurors will remember 65 percent of a demonstrative presentation after seventeen hours but only 10 percent of oral testimony alone (Poynter, 1987).

Clinical social workers have always used techniques that best fit the skills of their clients in order to assess, to form treatment plans, and to educate. We know better than anyone that it is often not enough to give a client bus money. You must draw a map, write down the bus number, mark the street numbers, and include landmarks.

Visual aids are stimulating and they are effective teaching tools. We are using the biopsychosocial assessment to inform the court. We want to help the judge or jury to visualize our findings whenever possible.

Computer technology is now helping medical doctors to show jurors the inner workings of the human body and the brain, and to demonstrate what happens when something goes wrong. In this way, they are able to take complex information and present it in a way that jurors can understand. Other forensic experts use the computer to simulate the trajectory of bullets, or to simulate car accidents or criminal assaults. Used appropriately, these tools are exciting and helpful simply because they are visual.

A software package is available for designing a genogram (family tree), which can be printed as a large chart to educate the jury regarding the family history of the client.

In preparation for court, I usually provide four or five charts that demonstrate my findings from the biopsychosocial assessment. Most judges allow me to step down from the witness stand and point to items on the chart for the jury. This is preferable to fumbling with overhead projectors, which are often not clear, or writing on a dry erase board and erasing the information. In most of my cases, the jury has been allowed to take the charts with them for deliberation or they have been left for the judge to peruse if needed. In some cases, a packet of materials on which I relied are prepared in visual form and given to the judge or the jury.

To highlight important points, color is used but not excessively. Much of the testimony from visual aids calls for narrative, but the opposing attorney often objects. It is important for the attorney to ask individual questions from the chart in order to elicit information you believe to be significant. I look forward to the time when a resourceful clinical social worker will design software that can animate child development stages and other life experiences that impact behavior.

EXAMPLES OF VISUAL AIDS

1. Childhood, adolescence, and adulthood themes or timelines
2. Psychological battering, and child abuse themes
3. Accumulation of factors that place children at risk
4. Post-traumatic stress disorder stages and symptoms
5. Genograms
6. Ecological charts that demonstrate support systems
7. Conclusions
8. Photographic enlargements of significant documents
9. Other photographs of people, places, or things
10. Crime statistics
11. Videotaped interviews or videos of communities
12. Maps or drawings of locations

EXAMPLE OF TESTIMONY USING VISUAL AIDS

Q. Ms. Vogelsang, do you have a chart that demonstrates what you learned about the Carter Training Schools that Mr. Jones attended?

A. Yes.

Q. Your honor, could Ms. Vogelsang step down from the witness stand please and review this chart for the jury?

A. Yes.

Q. Ms. Vogelsang, could you just begin by giving us an overview of this chart?

A. Yes, the chart shows the actual abuses found at the training school, and they are listed here as they were in the civil suit filed against the State of _____.

Q. And do you also have a complete copy of the civil suit with you here in court?

A. Yes, I do.

Q. And Ms. Vogelsang, how does this suit relate to the client in this case?

A. The client was incarcerated at this school at the time the abuses were occurring. He knew nothing about the existence of this suit, but described in some detail some of the incidences reported here. He witnessed some of the abuses of other children, and described some of the abuses that happened to him.

Q. Ms. Vogelsang, what is the significance of mixing a child like the defendant with children who are mentally ill?

A. He certainly would not have the skills to know how to handle relationships with those children. Sometimes their behavior was confusing to him, sometimes frightening. He could become extremely withdrawn himself or the very opposite—aggressive in an attempt to feel safe and establish his boundaries. Mr. Jones became extremely withdrawn and depressed, and began to look more like the children with whom he had been placed.

Q. And do the records indicate that he was placed with the emotionally disturbed children?

A. Yes.

Q. Do other staff at the school remember his placement with those children?

A. Yes.

Q. Was there ever any indication at all that Mr. Jones was emotionally disturbed when he was placed there?

A. No.

Q. Why was he put there?

A. According to the civil suit, it was typically due to poor assessments or no assessment, poor training of school staff, one psychologist per 300 juveniles, and overcrowding.

Q. Could you briefly review the other conditions listed on your chart that existed at this facility at this time?

A. Yes. Starting at the top of the chart you will see listed lack of proper ventilation in summer, lack of heat in winter, lack of proper fire safety equipment, roach-infested beds, inadequate nutrition, sexual abuse of inmates by guards, inadequate medical care, use of tear gas to control behavior, isolation without food for days at a time, and prohibition of communication with family, clergy, and others on the outside.

Q. And did Mr. Jones report to you that any of these conditions were present when he was at the training school?

A. Yes.

Q. And at the time of that interview, did Mr. Jones have any way of knowing that a suit had ever been filed?

A. Not that I could determine.

Although jurors may appear impassive, it is often difficult for them to hide their shock that such conditions exist, especially for children. To hear about it is one thing, but to see it in black and white or color is another. Jurors are sometimes taken to crime scenes so that they can have a better grasp of the details. Visual experience is definitely superior to listening to one expert after another drone on for hours.

After drawing your conclusions, consider what visual aids, if any, might help the court to understand the important points in your testimony.

VISUAL AIDS: SUMMARY

1. Begin assessing what types of visual aids would be appropriate to your case.
2. Begin recording information from your assessment either on the computer or on paper, and add to this as you gather more data.
3. Visual aids should highlight the most important points that you want to make in your testimony.
4. Make sure the charts are clear and readable.
5. Do not read every word on the chart. Be prepared to explain what is there and answer questions from the attorney.
6. If appropriate and aggreable to the attorney and the court, use a camcorder or photos to demonstrate your findings.

Chapter 10

Preparation of Testimony

It is difficult to imagine being unprepared for court. The experience is anxiety provoking enough when one is prepared, but to go into the courtroom cold does a disservice to the client and the court. One of the many advantages of the biopsychosocial assessment is that you begin identifying information that will be essential for testimony during the information-gathering stages. By the time you sit down to go over all the information, you already will have some ideas about the major themes in your case. You now have your interviews, your records, consultations with other experts, and publications and other literature.

THEMES, CONCLUSIONS, AND SOURCES

The first question to ask when preparing testimony is "What are the significant issues in this case?" Write them down, and then decide if they are consistent with information from the interviews, documents, and findings of others. If they are not consistent, then ask why. Usually, inconsistencies have shown up early and have been resolved during the information-gathering process.

The second question to pose is, "What are the conclusions up to this point?" Conclusions may change or be modified as the review of information continues, but draft them in some form from the start. After months of interviews, reading, researching, and talking with other experts, you should have an evolving list of possible conclusions ready to consider.

The third step in preparation is to go through the information and find the sources that support your conclusions. Be prepared to talk about those sources that do not support your conclusions and why. If five teachers stated that Johnny disrupted the classroom and one tells me that Johnny was the best student she ever had, I need to be able to account for the difference. This particular teacher may have had special skills for working with a child such as Johnny and simply found him easier to manage. You can bet that the opposing attorney will have information from that one teacher!

TELL THE ATTORNEY ABOUT YOUR OPINIONS

By the time I go to court, I have usually read my notes, the records, and the literature several times. If the attorney has met with me regularly and if he understands mental health issues, community issues, developmental issues, and so forth, then he will know what to ask and he will understand why it is important.

Some attorneys do not know much about mental health, child development, trauma, etc. This is why they bring in an expert. They must understand your findings in order to ask the appropriate questions. Meeting with attorneys before trials or hearings is crucial. Nothing is more anxiety provoking than being questioned on the stand by an attorney who asks questions that do not relate to the significant issues in your findings.

Once I have reviewed the materials yet again, established the themes of the material, and drafted some conclusions, it is time to write questions that I would ask of myself if the questioning were up to me. What needs to be asked in order to elicit the information relevant to the most important findings from the assessment? Should the conclusions be stated first or summarized later? Where in the testimony should the visual aids be placed? What questions should be asked about those visual aids? Share your views with the attorney.

PREPARING DIRECT AND CROSS-EXAMINATION

The office or your dining room can be a good place to set up a pretend courtroom. Visualize yourself on the stand, and run through your qualifying questions before reviewing questions for direct examination. The qualifying questions are a good warm-up and help to get you into the rhythm of your testimony. After two run-throughs, it is time to get into the direct testimony. Using the questions I have prepared, I ask each question out loud and then give my answers. It is important to assess whether or not the conclusions are clear and understandable, and whether the answers to my questions can be backed by at least two sources (Andrews, 1991). Two or three attempts at these questions usually begin to lower anxiety.

After going over the findings and the questions, it is important to anticipate cross-examination questions. What would I ask if I were cross-examining myself during my testimony? What information would I attack? Opposing attorneys often ask fair questions, questions that should be asked. I always want to be prepared to answer them openly and honestly. Cross-examination questions can be a wonderful opportunity to repeat or elaborate upon some of the information given during the direct examination, or to provide new information that did not come out of direct examination. Never go to court without trying to fairly challenge your own opinions.

Typically, you should run through your testimony at least three or four times during the week before court. Sometimes I will ask a friend to play attorney by asking the questions and then cross-examining me. Review your testimony again the night before and one more time the morning of the trial or hearing. Preparation reduces anxiety and provides the court with clear and comprehensible information. Some complain that this extensive practicing can make your testimony look rehearsed. Unless you have an incredibly wooden personality, it simply makes you look as if you have done your homework and can speak with confidence. The attorneys and other experts should be at home or in their offices doing the same thing!

PREPARATION OF TESTIMONY: SUMMARY

1. What are your themes?
2. What are your conclusions?
3. List the interviews you have done.
4. List the records you have reviewed.
5. List the experts you have consulted.
6. List the research you plan to use.
7. List preliminary visual aid possibilities.
8. Think of questions you might ask yourself.
9. Think about cross-examination questions you anticipate.
10. In order to feel confident, review your testimony.
11. Make sure you are qualified to discuss sanity and competency issues.

Chapter 11

Qualifying As an Expert

The ideal expert witness is a detective, a teacher, and an interpreter. This witness must teach the jurors because they are likely to ignore his opinion unless they can understand why he has formed it. He must also be an interpreter because scientific and technical terms have to be translated into language the jurors can understand and, by explaining the methodology of his investigation in a way that captures the jurors' interest, the expert can explain to the jurors why the opinion should be accepted.

Maryland Evidence Handbook
Second Edition
Murphy, 1993

For the clinical social worker, the qualification process is most important. Many of the questions asked will be the typical start-up questions. Some attorneys do not go much further than asking about your experience and training in specialty areas. Occasionally, the opposing attorney will object to my expertise, and unfortunately the attorney for the client cannot defend my expertise. This happens most often in family court. I have been qualified in areas in which I had no expertise because neither attorney had any idea what I really do. This typically happens with an attorney who says to you, "Oh, don't worry, I have qualified hundreds of experts. We do the school thing, the job thing, you know. No problem." This behavior is unacceptable from an attorney so do not go along with it.

Some of the start-up questions include:

1. Name
2. Education
3. Employment and work experience
4. Professional affiliations
5. License and certifications
6. Publications
7. Awards or achievements
8. Special appointments

Qualifying as an expert in conducting biopsychosocial assessments is especially important in terms of making sure that both the court and the opposing attorney know exactly what you do, when you do it, how you do it, why you do it, what others say about it, who accepts it, and why it is credible. If, as a clinical social worker, you choose to be qualified as an expert in some other area such as sexual abuse or mental retardation, it is still helpful to talk about the biopsychosocial assessment and the role it plays in your functioning as an expert in that area. For example:

> **Q.** As an expert in sexual abuse, do you use any sort of assessment tool or information-gathering process that you are specially trained to perform?
>
> **A.** Yes, the biopsychosocial assessment.
>
> **Q.** And what is a biopsychosocial assessment?
>
> **A.** The biopsychosocial assessment is . . .
>
> **Q.** And how is this assessment used in dealing with a case of sexual abuse?

Again, you are creating the opportunity to give information that would be much more narrow in focus if you were qualified as an expert in sexual abuse alone. Too often I have seen judges limit the testimony of a clinical social worker to the subject of sexual abuse without relating it to the particular client being treated. You are forced to speak in generalities rather than give the specifics as they relate to the person you have assessed.

In the qualifying process, you should clarify who clinical social workers are and what they do:

- We conduct biopsychosocial assessments and explain our finding to families, individuals, and groups as well as organizations such as the courts.
- We provide approximately 55 percent of all mental health treatment services in the United States.
- Twelve clinical social workers contributed to the DSM-IV.
- We are reimbursed by insurance companies for diagnosis and treatment.
- We work in a variety of settings including hospitals, agencies, businesses, private practices, etc.
- Other professionals rely on us to conduct biopsychosocial assessments.
- We are qualified as experts in family and criminal courts as well as in other legal settings, such as workers compensation or equity court.
- Our national office is located in Washington, DC, and we have over 100,000 members.
- The biopsychosocial assessment is a universally accepted tool in the profession of social work, and it is taught in every college of social work.

During the qualification process, you are educating the court on who you are and the importance of what you do. This critical stage sets a course for your testimony. Warning: *Never claim that you are expert in something that you cannot back up with your credentials and experience.*

SAMPLE OF QUALIFYING QUESTIONS FOR THE CLINICAL SOCIAL WORK EXPERT

The following is a sample of a complete qualification of a clinical social worker. It demonstrates the use of the biopsychosocial assessment as your expertise and can be used in most types of cases.

- Name
- Address
- Place of employment
- Nature of employment
- Specialty areas or other expertise
- Education
- License or certifications
- Special appointments
- Publications
- Achievements or awards
- Professional affiliations
- Other affiliations
- Duties and responsibilities with those affiliations
- Work experience
- Postgraduate training

At this point, the questioning regarding your expertise in conducting biopsychosocial assessments begins. You have already informed the jury about the specialty areas in your practice as well as your experience and expertise in those areas. Throughout my sample testimony, I make reference to experience and training I have in certain areas.

Q. As a master's (or doctorate) level clinical social worker, has your education included a procedure that is routinely accepted by family and criminal courts?

A. Yes. An integral part of the social work curriculum is learning to conduct biopsychosocial assessments that are used to impart information in a variety of settings including the courts.

Q. And what is a biopsychosocial assessment?

A. The biopsychosocial assessment is a social work procedure that is universally accepted in the field of social work as a method of gathering extensive information on an individual or family, and the environment and experiences of those persons. We use that information to explain that person's behavior and how it relates to his current situation. It will typically span three generations of family members. It is conducted through interviews with as many people as possible who have known the individual in any kind of significant way, a review of records or any documents that might substantiate the experiences in that individual's life, consultation with other experts involved with that individual, and review of any research or literature that might relate to that individual, his family, his environment, or situation. It often includes the use of visual aids to help in clarifying certain information that might be especially important.

Q. What is the purpose of doing all of this?

A. It helps to explain, not excuse, how an individual came to be in his or her current situation as it relates to the family's social, biological background, the environment, life experiences, and the person's development during exposure to these events.

Q. Why is it important to interview other people?

A. We do not grow up in a vacuum. Our lives are shaped by those who give birth to us and parent us. We are also shaped by teachers, friends, neighbors, and others. The many perspectives of others gives the social worker a way of checking for consistency of information, and a way of identifying family patterns of development and behavior.

Q. What kind of records do you typically get and why are they important?

A. Medical, psychological, school, social services court records, prison records, and many others. I try to obtain, or cause to be obtained, every piece of documentation ever generated on the individual and family members. These records provide additional information and help to substantiate the information from the interviews.

Q. Why do you interview other experts or professionals involved with the individual or family?

A. Not only is the information from other experts or professionals important in terms of gathering other opinions on the individual being assessed, but again to have another source other than interviews and records. Again, you are trying to find consistency in the information. For example, if the psychologist's testing results are in direct conflict with the observations or records of others, then it would be important to know why.

Q. Why does the biopsychosocial assessment require that you review research, journal articles, or other literature in assessing someone?

A. It is important to determine if there are any studies available, or if there are authors of research or other literature, and if their information relates in any way to the findings from interviews, records, and other experts. Again, with the biopsychosocial assessment, clinical social workers are drawing conclusions and expressing opinions based on a number of sources.

Q. Have you brought any visual aids to present to the court?

A. Yes.

Q. And could you explain to the court why those are part of the biopsychosocial assessment?

A. The use of visual aids to demonstrate significant issues or events related to the case helps to highlight the important findings from the assessment.

Q. And how is all of this helpful? How is it used?

A. It is most typically used in a variety of settings to explain the background and experiences of an individual, and how those relate to his current situation. In some settings, such as the courts, the information is given to the court in the form of testimony. In other settings, the information is used to form a plan for treatment or change.

Q. So, basically, you are doing what with all this information?

A. Explaining, based on volumes of information, how the person came to be where he is today, and if his situation is in any way related to his childhood history and the history of his family.

Q. What does the history of the family have to do with this individual you assessed?

A. It demonstrates patterns of behavior that might have influenced him during development. For example, if school records were to indicate that an unusual number of family members had learning problems, then we would also be alerted to the possibility that the client might also have had learning-related problems.

Q. How is biopsychosocial assessment different from the typical kind of diagnosing or testing done by psychiatrists, psychologists, or social workers in hospitals?

A. The information-gathering process is more in-depth. Where the state hospital or other agencies have biopsychosocial histories that are often one or two-page fill-in-the-blank type of questionnaires, a true biopsychosocial history will take an extensive amount of time depending on the nature of the case. Whereas the state hospital social worker or doctor may interview only the client and perhaps one other family member, the biopsychosocial assessment will include interviews with as many others as possible who knew the client, reviewing of hundreds of pages of documents on the client, and consulting with other experts along with a review of research.

Q. Why don't psychiatrists and psychologists do biopsychosocial assessments?

A. They are not trained to do clinical social work assessments.

Q. And do psychiatrists and psychologists routinely rely on clinical social workers to conduct these assessments and provide them with the information?

A. Yes.

Q. Are you familiar with the diagnostic and statistical manual used by mental health professionals to categorize emotional disorders?

A. Yes.

Q. Have any clinical social workers participated in the organizing and writing of this manual?

A. Yes. Twelve.

Q. Does a biopsychosocial assessment play any part in the diagnosing and treating of mental disorders?

A. Yes. Information from the assessment is generally placed on Axis IV under biopsychosocial stressors, but it is also used in diagnosing for the other four axes as well.

Q. What kind of training does a clinical social worker have to have to do an assessment such as this?

A. The two-year master's program at an accredited school of social work will have, as an integral part of its training, the methods for conducting these assessments. A significant part of our training is in gathering information and explaining what we have found to the courts and others. The training includes two internships in which hands-on experience is gained in addition to learning theory.

Q. How long have you been practicing social work and conducting these assessments?

A. Twenty-one years.

Q. And do you do this both in your private practice and when called upon by the courts?

A. Yes.

Q. Are licensed social workers reimbursed by insurance companies for diagnosing and treating various emotional problems?

A. Yes. And I would add that clinical social workers provide approximately 55 percent of all mental health services in the United States.

Q. Have you been qualified in any other courts as an expert in conducting biopsychosocial assessments and offering opinions based on your findings?

A. Yes, both in family and criminal court.

Q. In criminal cases, have you testified for the prosecution or the state as well as for the defense?

A. Yes.

Q. In what types of cases?

A. Child abuse, child custody, termination of parental rights, homicide, family violence cases, and criminal assault.

Q. Do you ever turn cases down?

A. Yes.

Q. Why?

A. Because the time required to conduct a thorough assessment is lengthy and limits the number that can be conducted for the court. I also have a private practice, and I limit the number of legal cases I assess.

Q. When do you agree to appear in court and give the information you have found through the biopsychosocial assessment?

A. Well, of course, if I am subpoenaed or court ordered to do so, I always attempt to comply. It is important to me professionally and ethically that there is enough time to do a thorough assessment, and that the information gathered is comprehensive enough to offer the court information that will be helpful in decision-making.

Q. Has any attorney decided not to use you because you were unable to gather adequate information to report to the court?

A. Yes.

Q. So, if you appear in court, it is because you believe that you have found information that would assist the court in making an informed decision?

A. Yes.

Q. Have you been called upon to testify in other states?

A. Yes.

Q. Were you qualified as an expert and asked to explain your findings to the court?

A. Yes.

Q. Were you asked to draw conclusions or render opinions as to how the information you gathered related to the current circumstances of the victim, client, defendant, etc.?

A. Yes.

The attorney then presents your curriculum vitae and asks the judge to qualify you as an expert in conducting biopsychosocial assessments and/or another area of expertise. Add your own questions regarding your other areas of expertise to this sample.

My experience has been that the opposing attorney usually challenges my expertise in conducting biopsychosocial assessments. But look at some typical objections.

> **Q.** You are not a doctor, are you?
> **A.** No.
> **Q.** You are not a psychologist or a psychiatrist, are you?
> **A.** No.
> **Q.** Is there any empirical evidence that supports your work?
> **A.** Yes.
> **Q.** So you are just a social worker, right?
> **A.** I am a master's level clinical social worker with twenty-one years of experience. (Do not sound defensive with this answer. Simply speak with confidence.)
> **Q.** (To the judge) Your Honor, I just don't understand. What she is an expert in? Is it social work?

Let's hope the judge has been listening and that the attorney can defend your expertise. You have made it quite clear.

> **JUDGE.** I am going to qualify this witness as an expert in conducting biopsychosocial assessments (and/or child welfare, trauma, mental retardation, etc.) and explaining her findings to the court. Please proceed.

Because so many judges and jurors continue to have a vague or incorrect perception of who social workers are and what they do, it is doubly important to make sure the court hears about your credibility as a witness. Even when the opposing attorney is willing to stipulate to your expertise, the attorney representing your client should complete the qualifying questions. Otherwise, the jury does not really know who you are and what you do, and why it is important to the case.

QUALIFYING AS AN EXPERT: SUMMARY

1. If you can qualify as an expert in a certain area, then do so. Consider whether that area will limit your testimony. Then consider the biopsychosocial assessment.
2. Review your qualifications, experience, and training. Make sure you are not claiming expertise in an area in which you are not qualified.
3. Be prepared to defend your expertise. Make sure the attorney is prepared to do so as well. Describe your expertise with confidence. Do not become angry or defensive.
4. Never assume that the attorney knows who you are, your area of expertise, or even understands your expertise.
5. Use the qualification process as an opportunity to make sure that the judge and jury know why you are there, and why your information is relevant.

Chapter 12

Direct Testimony

Remember that all parties including the judge, jury and opposing counsel will be evaluating you constantly. From the moment you appear, you will be under observation. You must, therefore, take great care in your appearance, manner and remarks at all times.

(Zaharris, 1997)

LAYING THE FOUNDATION

It is important for the clinical social worker to begin testimony with a detailed statement of exactly what she has done. She should give specific dates and times of interviews, both face-to-face and telephone interviews, each and every record reviewed, experts consulted and when, literature reviewed, and charts prepared. Some opposing attorneys will object to this detail or the judge may say, "OK, OK, we get the picture. Move on." At this point the attorney for the client will be thinking: "If I let her continue, it might anger the judge. What if the jurors are getting bored? What if they get ticked off?" One frustrating experience was during a case in which I listed the individuals I had interviewed, but I was cut off from explaining the amount of time spent in each interview. Later, a juror remarked that, even though a lot of people had been interviewed, there was no way the social worker could have spent enough time with each of them to learn very much. He had no way of knowing that ten to fifteen hours had been spent with each family member, and a minimum of three hours was spent with each person who was peripheral to the client's social network. Added to that, many hours had been spent reading records. Attorneys need to understand that we spend more time on assessment than other experts, and we probably know more about the client and his family than anyone else. It is important that the jury understands this as well. It does make a difference to detail the thoroughness of your assessment, and this is part of the mandate of the biopsychosocial assessment. It becomes even more significant when the opposing side is stating that it has its own assessments, which are typically one- or two-page fill-in-the-blank questionnaires drawn from one or two interviews.

When you stack a real biopsychosocial assessment conducted over days and months against a generic knee-jerk assessment that meets accreditation standards only, you are showing the thoroughness of your work. This overview of what you have done to prepare for court can be effective if the court has, up until that time, listened to opinions based on one or two interviews. They realize that you have indeed spent a lot of time with the people who are significant to the client, and you have been to their homes, their communities, their schools, and their doctors. You are giving them some firsthand information. The court responds to this type of testimony more than the technical, jargon-ridden information they receive from other experts. A very detailed direct examination that covers every conclusion in detail is my personal preference. Many attorneys strategize that some obvious information should deliberately be left out for the opposing attorney to jump on, thus deflecting him from inventing questions to confuse or entangle the witness. As a clinical social worker, I would rather reveal everything I know than deal with the tactical maneuvers favored by lawyers.

ADDRESSING THE COURT

During direct testimony, it is important to address the court and not the attorney. Because I have a private practice and I am accustomed to intense one-on-one communication, it is difficult for me to not answer an attorney's question directly. It is important to look at the judge, the attorneys, and the jury at various times during testimony. When discussing visual aids, the opposing attorneys usually walk over for a better view. Sometimes the judge will change his seating for a better view. It is important to try to address everyone in the courtroom, but try to direct most answers to the judge and the jury.

It is, of course, certainly appropriate to smile at certain times during a trial and to occasionally inject humor. But it is important to do so with caution. If there is any chance that a humorous remark might offend, do not make it. You do not know the jurors or their backgrounds, and you never know how your remarks may be interpreted. Humor can be offensive to those whose very serious situation is not at all funny to them, and it may be inconsiderate to a juror, the plaintiff, the victim, or the defendant. Those directly involved often complain of courtroom humor, rightfully so, during one of the most serious times of their lives. Zaharris recommends a "sober and formal appearance" (Zaharris, 1997).

During direct testimony, be sure to speak clearly, use language the jury can understand, and listen carefully to the questions asked. Speak slowly, but try to make your point within a reasonable amount of time. In his presentation to the NASW Annual Conference, Zaharris offered tips for being an effective witness (Zaharris, 1997). Some of the more helpful ones are reprinted here and should be reviewed before testifying. Additional tips can be found at the end of this presentation booklet and should also be reviewed prior to testimony:

1. Speak up so that all can hear you. Keep your hands away from your mouth. Answer each question with a verbal response. The court reporter transcribing your testimony cannot take down nods and shrugs.
2. Be polite. It is unlikely that you will be insulted or browbeaten, but if this seems to be happening, resist any urge to meet it with similar tactics. Even if the lawyer on the other side is acting outrageously, it will help your case if you maintain an attitude of courtesy and calm.
3. Do not be afraid to admit that you have had conferences with your lawyer (the client's lawyer) about the case. Every good

lawyer has conferences with his or her client. If examining counsel asks you, "Did your lawyer tell you what to say at this hearing?", you should answer truthfully and state that your lawyer (the client's lawyer) told you to tell the truth.

4. Avoid answering compound questions. Make the questioner split the question.

5. Avoid asking questions in your answers unless you are asking for a clarification of a question.

6. Do not look for traps in every question. There are not many trick questions, and if one comes along your counsel may help you out by objections or by other means. In trying to second guess each question, you will create the appearance of calculation, hesitation, or apprehension.

7. You must fight against showing any exasperation, boredom, or fatigue, even though the questioning may be very extensive. You will be protected by your counsel against harassment. Let your counsel know, however, if you feel ill or overly tired during the course of the examination. Your counsel can arrange for a short break or, if necessary, the adjournment of the hearing until another day.

8. Juries and judges associate with you—not with lawyers, who juries and judges expect will try to trick you with their questions.

9. Do not say "honestly," "truthfully," "candidly," etc. These are common figures of speech, but are inappropriate for testimony.

Many factors comprise judge, jury, and court decisions. You are not there to make or break the case. The outcome does not rest on your shoulders. Simply tell what you know, and relinquish any control you believe you have over the outcome. As a wise old judge once told me, "You did your best. I am the one who will have to lose sleep at night over my decisions."

DIRECT TESTIMONY: SUMMARY

1. Begin by giving details of what you have done in preparation for this testimony:

- Who you interviewed, when, how long.
- What records you reviewed.
- Which experts you contacted and how long you talked.
- What research you used in coming to your conclusions.
- What charts you have prepared.
2. Address the entire court, especially the judge and/or jury when testifying.
3. Use humor with caution.
4. Speak slowly and clearly.
5. Use language the jury can understand.
6. Always show respect to the court. Do not be sarcastic or flippant.
7. Speak with confidence.
8. Do not argue with the attorney or the judge.

Chapter 13

Cross-Examination

Why do trained social work professionals dread cross-examination with such fear and loathing? It has been proposed that we are used to being in positions of authority and control, and we do not like to have our opinions questioned. There is probably some truth to that theory, but most people are intimidated by the courtroom, especially the witness stand.

When I began as a caseworker in Los Angeles, the department had a half-day workshop on testifying in court. A judge came to speak to us about testimony. He instructed us to answer yes or no to most questions. In other words, do not elaborate because it gives the other attorney the opportunity to trap you. Now here we are, with the most detailed information on the client, and we are supposed to answer yes or no. This judge did make a statement that has stuck with me ever since. He told us that we were there simply to report what we had learned. We held no responsibility for the outcome of the case. He said that he had to take everything that was said in his courtroom, and grapple with each and every piece of information, then apply the law. He reassured us that it was not our fault if he took a position different from our opinions. It did not mean that our opinions were invalid, just that he had many considerations to view and that we must simply do the best we can. The rest was up to him. I found that enormously comforting: "Do the very best you can." I have tried to follow this simple advice and leave the rest to the court.

It is important to take your time on cross-examination. Never allow yourself to be rushed to answer. Do not be defensive. Some of the questions are quite good and should be asked. Because I can now anticipate good cross-examination questions, I prepare for them, but one can always be surprised by an unexpected question that requires consideration. Remember that material cannot be brought up on cross-examination if it was not brought up on direct examination (Hardwick, 1998). Do not take too long to answer. If you do not know the answer, say so. However, it is not wise to say, "I don't know" over and over again (Brodsky, 1991). When appropriate, I have explained that a particular question could best be answered by another expert on the case because it falls more clearly into her area of expertise.

THE MOST COMMONLY ASKED QUESTIONS ON CROSS-EXAMINATION

1. Who hired you?
2. How much are you being paid?
3. Do you belong to the Coalition to Abolish Fur Trapping?
4. How many times have you testified in this type of case?
5. Social work isn't really a science, is it?
6. Are your findings empirical?
7. You are not a medical doctor, now are you?
8. Nor a psychologist?
9. Nor a psychiatrist?

Good Answer: As I explained when I was qualified, I am a social worker with training and skills from a master's program and twenty-one years of experience in the field.

This reminds the jurors that you are not a non-social work trained caseworker with a vague background. Of course, by now they already know this from your qualifying questions and your direct testimony.

If the opposing attorney asks one of those "three-for-one" questions that are designed to confuse, ask her to break it down into individual questions. Unless they have written down the question, they can rarely repeat it and usually end up simplifying the question.

Never hesitate to ask that a question be repeated, or tell the attorney that you do not understand the question. Be sure not to do this so much that you appear dense or difficult!

Uncomfortable cross-examination experiences can be avoided if the attorneys for the client are paying attention to your testimony and remember to object. This, however, brings me to another big "don't." Never play attorney and signal the lawyer to react or make a comment about his lack of reaction. It can be hard to sit there and see a valuable piece of information go by the wayside because the attorney was not paying attention or did not grasp the moment for an objection. It is always best to let it go and look for a place later in your testimony to offer the information.

Hardwick reminds us that the attorney representing the side for which you are testifying will have the opportunity on redirect examination to counter any problems created during cross-examination (Hardwick, 1998). She also recommends that the witness state, "No, that is not true" in a polite way to the opposing attorney, if in fact that is the case.

EXAMPLES OF CROSS-EXAMINATION QUESTIONS

(Because attorneys have so much difficulty pronouncing my last name, I have tossed in a little humor here to lighten the load of cross-examination. These mispronunciations are real and make it difficult for me to keep a straight face at times.)

Q. Ms. Vogelsnag, have you ever been raped?
A. No.
Q. Ms. Vogelswag, were you sexually abused as a child?
A. No.
Q. Ms. Vagilsang, do you have children?
A. No.
Q. Ms. Bogeltree, how can you testify about parenting when you don't even have a child of your own?

A. While it is true that I have not had children, I have devoted my career to the protection of their rights, and after twenty-one years feel that they have taught me the things I need to know. I would add with all due respect, that I would not expect a cardiologist to have a heart attack in order to understand how to treat my heart problems.

Q. Ms. Vogelstein, could you conduct one of those psycho assessments on my dog?

A. You will have to make an appointment.

Most cross-examination questions are not tricky or designed to trap. Many are good, legitimate questions that we should ask of ourselves. We hope that the system is seeking the truth, and the truth should always be at the forefront of our responses.

CROSS-EXAMINATION: SUMMARY

1. Show respect for cross-examination questions.
2. Never play attorney by arguing a legal point.
3. If you do not understand the question, ask that it be repeated.
4. Look for opportunities to repeat information given on direct examination.
5. Answer "Yes" or "No" or "Although" or "While" before giving your explanation.
6. Do not rush to answer before the attorney finishes asking the question. Sometimes this requires great restraint!
7. Answer honestly. If you do not know the answer, say so. If the questions are more appropriate for another expert, state this to the court.
8. Anticipate cross-examination questions.
9. Remember that fees are paid for your work in assessing the client, not for your conclusions. Conclusions do not have a price attached.

Chapter 14

Courtroom Demeanor

The manner in which we conduct ourselves in the courtroom as well as our appearance affects the judge and the jury. Because we want to represent our profession well and show respect for the court, a number of do's and dont's must be considered.

Go to court in a suit. Choose something in muted colors that is understated and conservative. I try to avoid the stereotypical caricature of the social worker—the bun in the back of the head, blouse sticking out over the skirt, orthopedic shoes, and a raggedy briefcase. I have a great deal of respect for decorum in the courtroom, and I like judges who maintain strict rules on noise, sleeping, tank tops, and chewing gum.

Lay witnesses appear in court in some pretty wild garb, but I am always taken by surprise when I see an expert who dresses in poor taste. The following is a list of apparel to avoid in the courtroom.

1. Ponytails on men or women
2. Earrings for men or large dangly earrings on women
3. Rings on every finger or more than two fingers
4. Heavy makeup or "big hair" rooster styles
5. Barrettes, bows, headbands, or brightly colored clips
6. Loud prints, bold stripes, or acid-washed jeans
7. Miniskirts, slacks, or culottes
8. Tie-dye or hippie looks
9. Patterned pantyhose or socks, or ties with cartoons

Perhaps this seems overly rigid and conservative, but remember that your credibility is of ultimate importance in the courtroom.

Your appearance can influence people in a negative or positive way. You are also trying to act in the best interest of your client, and ethically you owe it to them to behave and dress professionally. Perhaps the day will come when courts are more casual and this information will seem silly. But we must operate within the context of the current courtroom rules.

Finally, I hate to say this, but please do not chew gum, twist your hair, bite your nails, wring you hands, fidget and twist, or engage in any other distracting nervous habits during your testimony. Again, you want the jury to listen to your testimony, not focus on your twitches and tics. Ask for water if your mouth feels dry. I always ask for a cup of water before I begin my testimony. I want to be as comfortable as possible on the stand.

Never forget that you are representing your entire profession, and your demeanor in the courtroom speaks for all social workers.

Appendix

Tips for Testifying in Court

TALK TO THE ATTORNEY ABOUT THE CASE

1. Communicate with the attorney frequently during the course of your case.
2. Ask yourself and the attorney if your expertise or information is appropriate for your case.
3. Ask the attorney what the themes and theories of the case are from his perspective.
4. Send your curriculum vitae; talk to the attorney about the social work profession; make sure the attorney understands who you are and what you do; tell him how you differ from a psychiatrist or psychologist.
5. Never accept the attorney's plan for qualifying you as an expert; write out the questions you believe should be asked to bring out your qualifications; anticipate cross-examination questions or objections to your qualifications, and make sure that you and the attorney can answer them.
6. If you receive a call from the opposing attorney seeking your opinions in a case, always politely refuse to discuss the case until you speak to the attorney representing your client.
7. Do not let the attorney bully, intimidate, or charm you into expressing opinions you do not hold and cannot back.
8. Be careful what you put into writing in affidavits, reports, or communications to attorneys. These materials may be subject to discovery. Make sure you can support anything you put into writing.

PREPARATION

1. Preparation is the key to success on the witness stand and it also lowers anxiety.
2. Make a list of your opinions and conclusions.
3. Make sure you can support each claim you want to make with:

- Your clinical training, experience, and skills
- Records and documents
- Information from other experts
- Affidavits obtained by the attorney
- Facts of the case
- Two or more sources for each piece of information given in testimony.

4. Write questions that you believe would best bring out the information you want to impart.
5. Anticipate cross-examination questions and be prepared to answer them.
6. Have a friend ask you these questions and do two or three runthroughs before going to court.
7. Ask the attorney representing your case to describe the style of the opposing attorney.
8. Read your testimony from other cases or that of other experts in similar cases. This is a great learning tool.

ON THE WITNESS STAND

1. Dress in a comfortable suit; muted tones are best.
2. Do not fraternize with others at the courthouse before testifying.
3. Be aware of what you take to the stand; discuss materials with the attorney before going on the stand.
4. Listen carefully to questions and pause for three seconds before answering.
5. Ask for water if you need it.
6. Look first at the attorney and then at the jury when answering questions.
7. Never act angry, defensive, or sarcastic. Always remain calm, patient, and unflappable, yet confident, no matter what is thrown your way.
8. If there is an objection, stop answering and allow the attorneys time to resolve the objection. Never try to interrupt and explain.
9. If the attorneys approach the bench to confer with the judge, look away and try not to listen.
10. Answer questions with "yes or no," "although and while," "to the contrary," "that is not how it is at all," and then give your explanation.
11. It is acceptable to say "I don't know," or "I don't remember," but if you respond this way too frequently, your credibility may be affected depending on the nature of the case.

12. Use humor sparingly or not at all.
13. Courtrooms can be hot, cold, stuffy, and moldy. If you are going to be on the stand for awhile, make sure you are wearing clothes that allow the removal of a jacket.
14. Follow carefully any judge's instructions not to discuss the case during breaks in the proceedings.
15. Take time before and after the trial to relax and relieve stress.

Bibliography

American Jurisprudence Proof of Facts (1997). *Child neglect.* 3POF, Second edition. New York: Lawyers Cooperative Publishing.

American Psychiatric Association (1994). *Diagnostic and statistical manual of mental disorders,* Fourth edition. Washington, DC: American Psychiatric Association.

Andrews, Arlene (1991). Social work expert testimony regarding mitigation in capital sentencing proceedings. *Social Work, 36*(5), 440-445.

Barker, Robert L. and Branson, Douglas M. (1993). *Forensic social work: Legal aspects of professional practice.* Binghamton, New York: The Haworth Press, Inc.

Brill, Miriam and Taler, Aviva (1990). A spiral model for teaching biopsychosocial assessment. *Journal of Teaching in Social Work, 4*(1), 67-82.

Brodsky, Stanley L. (1991). *Testifying in court: Guidelines and maxims for the expert witness.* Washington, DC: American Psychological Association.

Copeland, Edna and Love, Valerie (1995). *Attention, please! A comprehensive guide for successfully parenting children with attention disorders and hyperactivity.* Plantation, Florida: Specialty Press, Inc.

Gifis, Steven H. (1991). *Law dictionary,* Third edition. New York: Barron's.

Hardwick, Charlotte (1998). *Witness Guide or Deposition or Court: How to Give Testimony in Any Kind of Case.* Livingston, Texas: Pale Horse Publishing.

Herman, Judith (1992). *Trauma and recovery.* USA: BasicBooks.

Karls, James and Wandrei, Karen (1994). *Person-in-environment system: The PIE classification system for social functioning problems.* Washington, DC: NASW Press.

Lazarus, Arnold A. (1989). *The practice of multimodal therapy.* Baltimore: The Johns Hopkins University Press.

Luckkason, Ruth and Ellis, James (1985). Mentally retarded criminal defendants. *Mental Retardation and Criminal Defense, 53*(3/4), 414-493.

Lukas, Susan (1993). *Where to start and what to ask: An Assessment Handbook.* New York: W. W. Norton and Company.

Murphy, Joseph (1993). *Maryland evidence handbook,* Second edition, 1400 at 703.

National Association of Social Workers Delegate Assembly (1996). *Code of Ethics,* Revised edition. Washington, DC: NASW.

Poynter, Dan (1987). *The expert witness handbook: Tips and techniques for the litigation consultant.* Santa Barbara, California: Para Publishing.

Rogers, Richard (Ed.) (1997). *Clinical assessment of malingering and deception.* Second edition. New York: Guilford Press.

van der Kolk, Bessel A. (1988). The trauma spectrum: The interaction of biological and social events in the genesis of the trauma response. *Journal of Traumatic Stress, 1*(3), 273-290.

Zaharris, Drake (1997). Social workers as expert witnesses. Presentation for National Association of Social Workers Annual Conference, Baltimore, Maryland, October 5, 1997.

Index

Page numbers followed by the letter "e" indicate examples.

HAWORTH Social Work Practice in Action
Carlton E. Munson, PhD, Senior Editor

DIAGNOSIS IN SOCIAL WORK: NEW IMPERATIVES by Francis J. Turner. (2002).

HUMAN BEHAVIOR IN THE SOCIAL ENVIRONMENT: INTERWEAVING THE INNER AND OUTER WORLD by Esther Urdang. (2002).

THE USE OF PERSONAL NARRATIVES IN THE HELPING PROFESSIONS: A TEACHING CASEBOOK by Jessica Heriot and Eileen J. Polinger. (2002).

CHILDREN'S RIGHTS: POLICY AND PRACTICE by John T. Pardeck. (2001) "Courageous and timely . . . a must-read for everyone concerned not only about the rights of America's children but also about their fate." *Howard Jacob Kerger, PhD, Professor and PhD Director, University of Houston Graduate School of Social Work, Texas*

BUILDING ON WOMEN'S STRENGTHS: A SOCIAL WORK AGENDA FOR THE TWENTY-FIRST CENTURY, SECOND EDITION by K. Jean Peterson and Alice A. Lieberman. (2001).

ELEMENTS OF THE HELPING PROCESS: A GUIDE FOR CLINICIANS, SECOND EDITION by Raymond Fox. (2001).

SOCIAL WORK THEORY AND PRACTICE WITH THE TERMINALLY ILL, SECOND EDITION by Joan K. Parry. (2000). "Timely . . . a sensitive and practical approach to working with people with terminal illness and their family members." *Jeanne A.Gill, PhD, LCSW, Adjunct Faculty, San Diego State University, California, and Vice President Southern California Chapter, AASWG*

WOMEN SURVIVORS, PSYCHOLOGICAL TRAUMA, AND THE POLITICS OF RESISTANCE by Norma Jean Profitt. (2000). "A compelling argument on the importance of political and collective action as a means of resisting oppression. Should be read by survivors, service providers, and activists in the violence-against-women movement." *Gloria Geller, PhD, Faculty of Social Work, University of Regina, Saskatchewan, Canada*

THE MENTAL HEALTH DIAGNOSTIC DESK REFERENCE: VISUAL GUIDES AND MORE FOR LEARNING TO USE THE DIAGNOSTIC AND STATISTICAL MANUAL (DSM-IV) by Carlton E. Munson. (2000). "A carefully organized and user-friendly book for the beginning student and less-experienced practitioner of social work, clinical psychology, of psychiatric nursing . . . It will be a valuable addition to the literature on clinical assessment of mental disorders." *Jerold R. Brandell, PhD, BCD, Professor, School of Social Work, Wayne State University, Detroit, Michigan and Founding Editor, Psychoanalytic Social Work*

HUMAN SERVICES AND THE AFROCENTRIC PARADIGM by Jerome H. Schiele. (2000). "Represents a milestone in applying the Afrocentric paradigm to human services generally, and social work specifically. . . . A highly valuable resource." *Bogart R. Leashore, PhD, Dean and Professor, Hunter College School of Social Work, New York, New York*

SOCIAL WORK: SEEKING RELEVANCY IN THE TWENTY-FIRST CENTURY by Roland Meinert, John T. Pardeck and Larry Kreuger. (2000). "Highly recommended. A thought-provoking work that asks the difficult questions and challenges the status quo. A great book for graduate students as well as experienced social workers and educators." *Francis K. O. Yuen, DSW, ACSE, Associate Professor, Division of Social Work, California State University, Sacramento*

SOCIAL WORK PRACTICE IN HOME HEALTH CARE by Ruth Ann Goode. (2000). "Dr. Goode presents both a lucid scenario and a formulated protocol to bring health care services into the home setting. . . . this is a must have volume that will be a reference to be consulted many times." *Marcia B. Steinhauer, PhD, Coordinator and Associate Professor, Human Services Administration Program, Rider University, Lawrenceville, New Jersey*

FORSENIC SOCIAL WORK: LEGAL ASPECTS OF PROFESSIONAL PRACTICE, SECOND EDITION by Robert L. Barker and Douglas M. Branson. (2000). "The authors combine their expertise to create this informative guide to address legal practice issues facing social workers." *Newsletter of the National Organization of Forensic Social Work*

SOCIAL WORK IN THE HEALTH FIELD: A CARE PERSPECTIVE by Lois A. Fort Cowles. (1999). "Makes an important contrition to the field by locating the practice of social work in health care within an organizational and social context." *Goldie Kadushin, PhD, Associate Professor, School of Social Welfare, University of Wisconsin, Milwaukee*

SMART BUT STUCK: WHAT EVERY THERAPY NEEDS TO KNOW ABOUT LEARNING DISABILITIES AND IMPRISONED INTELLIGENCE by Myrna Orenstein. (1999). "A trailblazing effort that creates an entirely novel way of talking and thinking about learning disabilities. There is simply nothing like it in the field." *Fred M. Levin, MD, Training Supervising Analyst, Chicago Institute for Psychoanalysis; Assistant Professor of Clinical Psychiatry, Northwestern University, School of Medicine, Chicago, IL*

CLINICAL WORK AND SOCIAL ACTION: AN INTEGRATIVE APPROACH by Jerome Sachs and Fred Newdom. (1999). "Just in time for the new millennium come Sachs and Newdom with a wholly fresh look at social work. . . . A much-needed uniting of social work values, theories, and practice for action." *Josephine Nieves, MSW, PhD, Executive Director, National Association of Social Workers*

SOCIAL WORK PRACTICE IN THE MILITARY by James G. Daley. (1999). "A significant and worthwhile book with provocative and stimulating ideas. It deserves to be read by a wide audience in social work education and practice as well as by decision makers in the military." *H. Wayne Johnson, MSW, Professor, University of Iowa, School of Social Work, Iowa City, Iowa*

GROUP WORK: SKILLS AND STRATEGIES FOR EFFECTIVE INTERVEN-TIONS, SECOND EDITION by Sondra Brandler and Camille P. Roman. (1999). "A clear, basic description of what group work requires, including what skills and techniques group workers need to be effective." *Hospital and Community Psychiatry* (from the first edition)

TEENAGE RUNAWAYS: BROKEN HEARTS AND "BAD ATTITUDES" by Laurie Schaffner. (1999). "Skillfully combines the authentic voice of the juvenile runaway with the principles of social science research."

CELEBRATING DIVERSITY: COEXISTING IN A MULTICULTURAL SOCIETY by Benyamin Chetkow-Yanoov. (1999). "Makes a valuable contribution to peace theory and practice." *Ian Harris, EdD, Executive Secretary, Peace Education Committee, International Peace Research Association*

SOCIAL WELFARE POLICY ANALYSIS AND CHOICES by Hobart A. Burch. (1999). "Will become the landmark text in its field for many decades to come." *Sheldon Rahan, DSW, Founding Dean and Emeritus Professor of Social Policy and Social Administration. Faculty of Social Work, Wilfrid Laurier University, Canada*

SOCIAL WORK PRACTICE: A SYSTEMS APPROACH, SECOND EDITION by Benyamin Chetkow-Yannov. (1999). "Highly recommended as a primary text for any and all introductory social work courses." *Ram A. Cnaan, PhD, Associate Professor, School of Social Work, University of Pennsylvania*

CRITICAL SOCIAL WELFARE ISSUES: TOOLS FOR SOCIAL WORK AND HEALTH CARE PROFESSIONALS edited by Arthur J. Katz, Abraham Lurie, and Carlos M. Vida. (1997). "Offers hopeful agendas for change, while navigating the societal challenges facing those in the human services today." *Book News Inc.*

SOCIAL WORK IN HEALTH SETTINGS: PRACTICE IN CONTEXT, SECOND EDITION edited by Tobra Schwaber Kerson. (1997). "A first-class document . . . It will be found among the steadier and lasting works on the social work aspects of American health care." *Hans S. Falck, PhD, Professor Emeritus and Former Chair, Health Specialization in Social Work, Virginia Commonwealth University*

PRINCIPLES OF SOCIAL WORK PRACTICE: A GENERIC PRACTICE AP-PROACH by Molly R. Hancock. (1997). "Hancock's discussions advocate reflection and self-awareness to create a climate for client change." *Journal of Social Work Education*

NOBODY'S CHILDREN: ORPHANS OF THE HIV EPIDEMIC by Steven F. Dansky. (1997). "Professional sound, moving, and useful for both professionals and interested readers alike." *Ellen G. Friedman, ACSW, Associate Director of Support Services, Beth Israel Medical Center, Methadone Maintenance Treatment Program*

SOCIAL WORK APPROACHES TO CONFLICT RESOLUTION: MAKING FIGHTING OBSOLETE by Benyamin Chetkow-yanoov. (1996). "Presents an examination of the nature and cause of conflict and suggests techniques for coping with conflict." *Journal of Criminal Justice*

FEMINIST THEORIES AND SOCIAL WORK: APPROACHES AND APPLICA-TIONS by Christine Flynn Salunier. (1996). "An essential reference to be read repeatedly by all educators and practitioners who are eager to learn more about feminist theory and practice" *Nancy R. Hooyman, PhD, Dean and Professor, School of Social Work, University of Washington, Seattle*

THE RELATIONAL SYSTEMS MODEL FOR FAMILY THERAPY: LIVING IN THE FOUR REALITIES by Donald R. Bardill. (1996). "Engages the reader in quiet, thoughtful conversation on the timeless issue of helping families and individuals." *Christian Counseling Resource Review*

SOCIAL WORK INTERVENTION IN AN ECONOMIC CRISIS: THE RIVER COMMUNITIES PROJECT by Martha Baum and Pamela Twiss. (1996). "Sets a standard for universities in terms of the types of meaningful roles they can play in supporting and sustaining communities." *Kenneth J. Jaros, PhD, Director, Public Health Social Work Training Program, University of Pittsburgh*

FUNDAMENTALS OF COGNITIVE-BEHAVIOR THERAPY: FROM BOTH SIDES OF THE DESK by Bill Borcherdt. (1996). "Both beginning and experienced practitioners . . . will find a considerable number of valuable suggestions in Borcherdt's book." *Albert Ellis, PhD, President, Institute for Rational-Emotive Therapy, New York City*

BASIC SOCIAL POLICY AND PLANNING: STRATEGIES AND PRACTICE METHODS by Hobart A. Burch. (1996). "Burch's familiarity with his topic is evident and his book is an easy introduction to the field." *Readings*

THE CROSS-CULTURAL PRACTICE OF CLINICAL CASE MANAGEMENT IN MENTAL HEALTH edited by Peter Manoleas. (1996). "Makes a contribution by bringing together the cross-cultural and clinical case management perspectives in working with those who have serious mental illness." *Disabilities Studies Quarterly*

FAMILY BEYOND FAMILY: THE SURROGATE PARENT IN SCHOOLS AND OTHER COMMUNITY AGENCIES by Sanford Weinstein. (1995). "Highly recomended to anyone concerned about the welfare of our children and the breakdown of the American family." *Jerold S. Greenberg, EdD, director of Community Service, College of Health & Human Performance, University of Maryland*

PEOPLE WITH HIV AND THOSE WHO HELP THEM: CHALLENGES, INTEGRATION, INTERVENTION by R. Dennis Shelby. (1995). "A useful and compassionate contribution to the HIV psychotherapy literature." *Public Health*

THE BLACK ELDERLY: SATISFACTION AND QUALITY OF LATER LIFE by Marguerite Coke and James A. Twaite. (1995). "Presents a model for predicting life satisfaction in this population." *Abstracts in Social Gerontology*

BUILDING ON WOMEN'S STRENGTHS: A SOCIAL WORK AGENDA FOR THE TWENTY-FIRST CENTURY edited by Liane V. Davis. (1994). "The most lucid and accessible overview of the related epistemological debates in the social work literature." *Journal of the National Association of Social Workers*

NOW DARE EVERYTHING: TALES OF HIV-RELATED PSYCHOTHERAPY by Steven F. Dansky. (1994). "A highly recommended book for anyone working with persons who are HIV positive. . . . Every library should have a copy of this book." *AIDS Book Review Journal*

INTERVENTION RESEARCH: DESIGN AND DEVELOPMENT FOR HUMAN SERVICE edited by Jack Rothman and Edwin J. Thomas. (1994). "Provides a useful framework for the further examination of methodology for each separate step of such research." *Academic Library Book Review*

CLINICAL SOCIAL WORK SUPERVISION, SECOND EDITION by Carlton E. Munson. (1993). "A useful, thorough, and articulate reference for supervisors and for 'supervisees' who are wanting to understand their supervisor or are looking for effective supervision...." *Transactional Analysis Journal*

ELEMENTS OF THE HELPING PROCESS: A GUIDE FOR CLINICIANS by Raymond Fox. (1993). "Filled with helpful hints, creative interventions, and practical guidelines." *Journal of Family Psycotherapy*

IF A PARTNER HAS AIDS: GUIDE TO CLINICAL INTERVENTION FOR RELATIONSHIPS IN CRISIS by R. Dennis Shelby. (1993). "A women addition to existing publications about couples coping with AIDS, it offers intervention ideas and strategies to clinicians." *Contemporary Psychology*

GERONTOLOGICAL SOCIAL WORK SUPERVISION by Ann Burack-Weiss and Frances Coyle Brennan. (1991). "The creative ideas in this book will aid supervisiors working with students and experienced social workers." *Senior News*

THE CREATIVE PRACTITIONER: THEORY AND METHODS FOR THE HELPING SERVICES by Bernard Gelfand. (1988). "[Should] be widely adopted by those in the helping services. It could lead to significant positive advances by countless individuals." *Sidney J. Parnes, Trustee Chairperson for Strategic Program Development, Creative Education Foundation, Buffalo, NY*

MANAGEMENT AND INFORMATION SYSTEMS IN HUMAN SERVICES: IMPLICATIONS FOR THE DISTRIBUTION OF AUTHORITY AND DECISION MAKING by Richard K. Caputo. (1987). "A contribution to social work scholarship in that it provides conceptual frameworks that can be used in the design of management information systems." *Social Work*

Order Your Own Copy of
This Important Book for Your Personal Library!

THE WITNESS STAND
A Guide for Clinical Social Workers in the Courtroom

_____in hardbound at $29.95 (ISBN: 0-7890-1144-1)
_____in softbound at $19.95 (ISBN: 0-7890-1145-X)

COST OF BOOKS_____	❏ **BILL ME LATER:** ($5 service charge will be added)
	(Bill-me option is good on US/Canada/Mexico orders only; not good to jobbers, wholesalers, or subscription agencies.)
OUTSIDE USA/CANADA/ MEXICO: ADD 20%____	
	❏ Check here if billing address is different from shipping address and attach purchase order and billing address information.
POSTAGE & HANDLING_____	
(US: $4.00 for first book & $1.50 for each additional book)	
Outside US: $5.00 for first book & $2.00 for each additional book)	
	Signature_____
SUBTOTAL_____	❏ **PAYMENT ENCLOSED: $**_____
in Canada: add 7% GST____	❏ **PLEASE CHARGE TO MY CREDIT CARD.**
STATE TAX____	❏ Visa ❏ MasterCard ❏ AmEx ❏ Discover
(NY, OH & MIN residents, please add appropriate local sales tax)	❏ Diner's Club ❏ Eurocard ❏ JCB
	Account # _____
FINAL TOTAL____	
(If paying in Canadian funds, convert using the current exchange rate, UNESCO coupons welcome.)	Exp. Date_____
	Signature_____

Prices in US dollars and subject to change without notice.

NAME_____

INSTITUTION_____

ADDRESS_____

CITY_____

STATE/ZIP_____

COUNTRY_____ COUNTY (NY residents only)_____

TEL_____ FAX_____

E-MAIL_____

May we use your e-mail address for confirmations and other types of information? ❏ Yes ❏ No
We appreciate receiving your e-mail address and fax number. Haworth would like to e-mail or fax special discount offers to you, as a preferred customer. **We will never share, rent, or exchange your e-mail address or fax number.** We regard such actions as an invasion of your privacy.

Order From Your Local Bookstore or Directly From
The Haworth Press, Inc.
10 Alice Street, Binghamton, New York 13904-1580 • USA
TELEPHONE: 1-800-HAWORTH (1-800-429-6784) / Outside US/Canada: (607) 722-5857
FAX: 1-800-895-0582 / Outside US/Canada: (607) 722-6362
E-mail: getinfo@haworthpressinc.com
PLEASE PHOTOCOPY THIS FORM FOR YOUR PERSONAL USE.
www.HaworthPress.com

BOF00